CARMARTHEN
THROUGH TIME
Keith E. Morgan

AMBERLEY

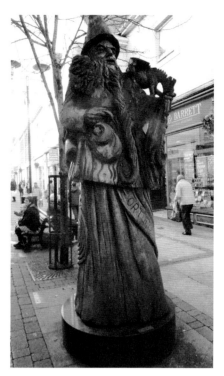
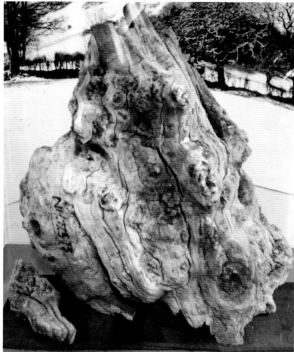

Merlin the Wizard

A wooden sculpture of Merlin, the wizard of Arthurian legend, on Merlin's Walk in Carmarthen. Sculptured by Simon Hedger, Merlin the Wizard was unveiled by the mayor of Carmarthen on 10 April 2010. One variation of the Arthurian legend has it that Merlin was born in a cave outside Carmarthen and given that the Welsh version of the town's name is Caerfyrddin, some say that Merlin is an anglicised version of Myrddin. The statue of Merlin was carved from a tree felled to make way for a new shopping centre in the town and is symbolic of the mythical Merlin's Oak, a tree that once stood in the older part of Carmarthen. Legend has it that once Merlin's Oak fell, so would Carmarthen. The tree died some years ago and its remains are preserved in Carmarthen Museum. Needless to say, Carmarthen is still here – so much for legend.

This book is dedicated in memory of Malvina, 'My Special Angell'.

First published 2016

Amberley Publishing
The Hill, Stroud, Gloucestershire, GL5 4EP
www.amberley-books.com

Copyright © Keith E. Morgan, 2016

The right of Keith E. Morgan to be identified as the Author of this work has been asserted in accordance with the Copyrights, Designs and Patents Act 1988.

ISBN 978 1 4456 5277 1 (print)
ISBN 978 1 4456 5278 8 (ebook)

British Library Cataloguing in Publication Data.
A catalogue record for this book is available from the British Library.

Typesetting by Amberley Publishing.
Printed in Great Britain.

Introduction

Carmarthen, the county town of Carmarthenshire, claims to be the oldest town in Wales. Its roots go back to the Roman occupation when Carmarthen was the civitas capital of the Celtic Demetae (Britons) tribe and known as Moridunum (sea fort). The Roman fort in the town dates from around AD 75 and was recorded by Ptolemy and the Antonine Itinerary. Near the fort, and excavated in 1968 is one of only three surviving Roman amphitheatres found in Wales (the other two being at Caerleon and Tomen-y-Mur). During the Middle Ages, the settlement was known as Llanteulyddog (St Teulyddog's). There are strong Arthurian legends connecting Merlin with Carmarthen, but it was the town's strategic importance that was recognised by the Norman William Fitz Baldwin who built a castle here around 1094. The castle was destroyed by Llywelyn the Great in 1215 and rebuilt in 1223, the same time as the town walls were constructed making Carmarthen one of the first walled towns in Wales. Neither of these defences prevented Owain Glyndŵr from sacking both town and castle in 1405. During the Civil War in the 1640s, the town was enclosed by new walls known as the Bulwarks, the remains of which can be seen near the police headquarters and are considered to be the best surviving examples of Royalist Civil War town fortifications in Britain. In the sixteenth and seventeenth centuries, Carmarthen rose to prominence as a business centre for agriculture and associated trades, including woollen manufacture. On the site of what was the former church of St Mary and completed in 1777, the guildhall dates from at least the sixteenth century. The eighteenth century saw Carmarthen enter the industrialised age. Coal, iron and tinplate trades became important and, as a port, Carmarthen exported its products throughout the world. Today, the former cattle market in the heart of the town has undergone regeneration and Carmarthen has become a large business and shopping centre for the county.

Keith E. Morgan

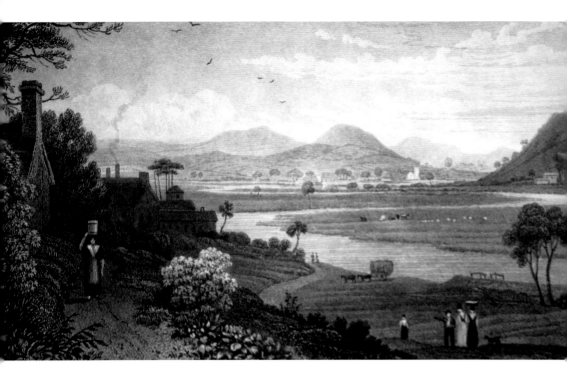

The Vale of the Towy and Merlin's Hill

Two views, one print and one photograph, looking north-east from what is now The Parade, up the Vale of the Towy to Merlin's Hill. The print is from an antique line engraving by T. Ba after Henry Gastineau, *c.* 1835, and coloured by hand. The photograph from roughly the same location was taken from a postcard franked 31 May 1909.

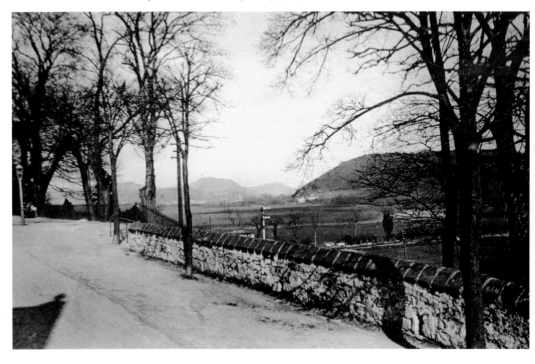

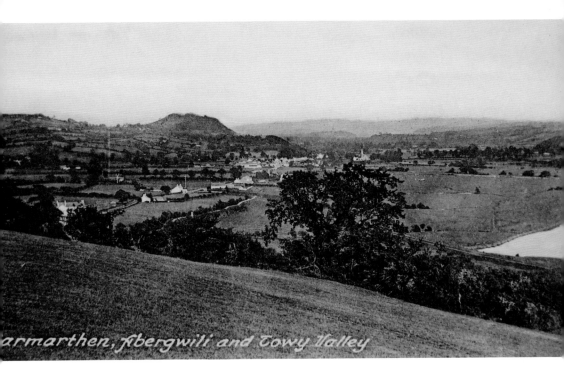

armarthen, Abergwili and Towy Valley

The Vale of Towy, Abergwili and Merlin's Hill

The top photograph, printed as a postcard and dated roughly to the early 1900s, was probably taken from the hillside above Tarnedy, north-east of Carmarthen, and shows the floodplain where the Rivers Gwili and Towy converge just south of the village of Abergwili with Merlin's Hill in the background, brooding over the whole scene. The lower picture is a view taken from the summit of Merlin's Hill on 31 October 2015, looking in the opposite direction downstream towards Carmarthen.

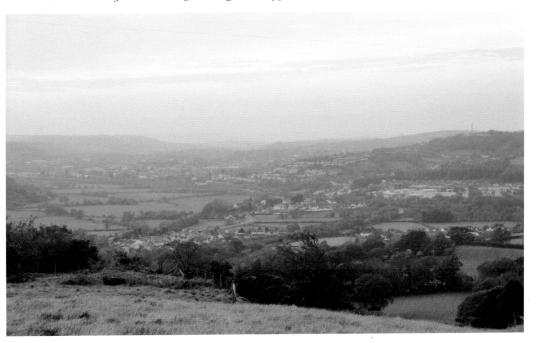

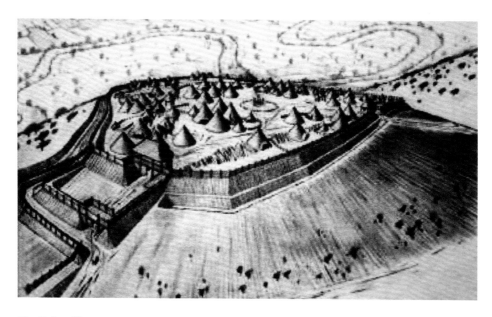

Merlin's Hill

An artist's impression of how the Iron Age hill fort on Merlin's Hill would have probably looked like to the Romans when they occupied South Wales in AD 75. Viewed from the north, where the main entrance to the hill fort was situated, the illustration is by designer Phillip Wait and kindly provided by the Cambria Archaeology/Dyfed Archaeological Trust. The hill fort itself dates back to around 400 BC and was occupied by the Celtic Demetae/Britons Tribe. Unlike their more aggressive neighbours to the west, the Silures, the Demetae Tribe appeared to have been relatively comfortable with their Roman client status. The tribe was granted civitas status with a capital at Moridunum Demetarum (British Caerfyrddin, or modern Carmarthen). To give an idea of the scale of the hill fort, in the bottom photograph the author is standing in front of the raised escarpments comprising part of the formidable north entrance to the encampment.

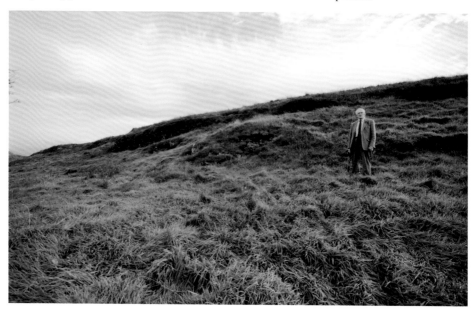

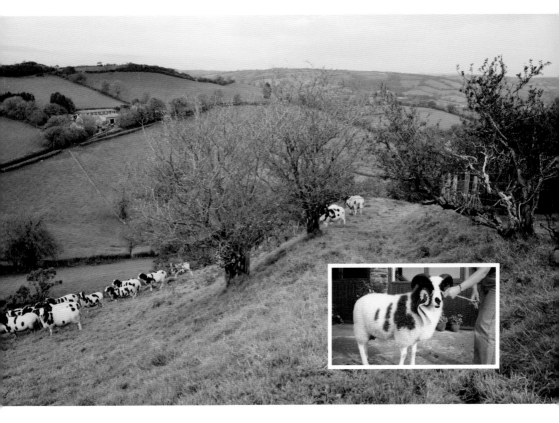

Merlin's Hill

Legends of Merlin abound in the Carmarthen area. Merlin's Hill is no exception and has acquired one all of its own. In 1188, Gerald Cambrensis (also known as Gerald of Wales) wrote that Merlin was born in Carmarthen. Merlin the Wizard, who was King Arthur's guardian and possessed magical powers, is believed to have lived in a cave in Merlin's Hill. This cave was to serve both as his home and tomb, and according to legend he was locked there in bonds of enchantment by his lover. The whereabouts of the cave have long been lost with the passage of time and the only ones that hear Merlin clanking his chains today are the flocks of Jacob sheep who roam freely over these lonely heights. The flocks all belong to Sharon and Gareth Richards of Alltyfyrddin Farm, Abergwili. The photograph of the Jacob ram (inset), Myrddin Caradog, was taken after he had been shown by his owner, ten-year-old Carwyn Richards, at the 2003 United Counties Show at Carmarthen and being awarded Reserve Champion of the Jacob sheep section.

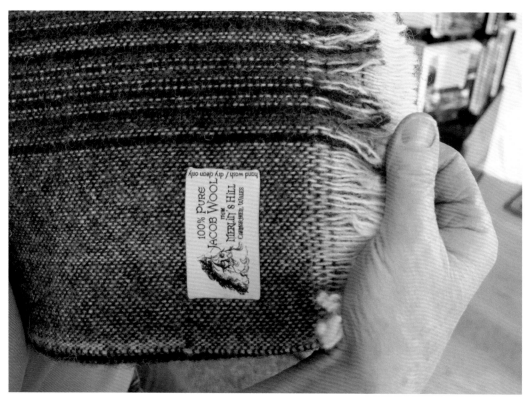

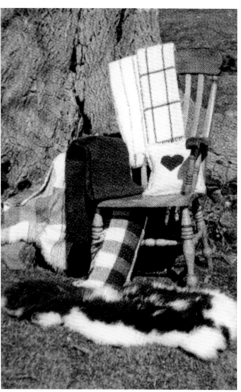

Merlin's Hill

Well worth a visit is the Merlin's Hill Centre at Alltyfyrddin Farm, Abergwili, which is located under the overpowering shadow of the Iron Age hill fort on top of Merlin's Hill. The Carmarthenshire farm enterprise is run by the NFU/Natwest Wales Woman Farmer of 2004, Sharon Richards. She was also nominated to be Farming Ambassador of the Year in Wales for the work that she has done in conceiving the Merlin's Hill Centre and bringing it to life as a visitor attraction. The 220-acre farm straddles the Iron Age hill fort and as well as maintaining a 200-strong dairy herd, 120 purebred Jacob sheep are allowed to roam free over its ramparts. The woollen trade was very important to Carmarthen in the Middle Ages and beyond and the Jacob sheep have provided a revival of this once traditional trade. The two photographs serve to show how the characteristic shades of grey and brown wool from the Jacob sheep are woven to make blankets, throws and scarves for sale at the Merlin's Hill Wool Collection run by daughter Carys Richards.

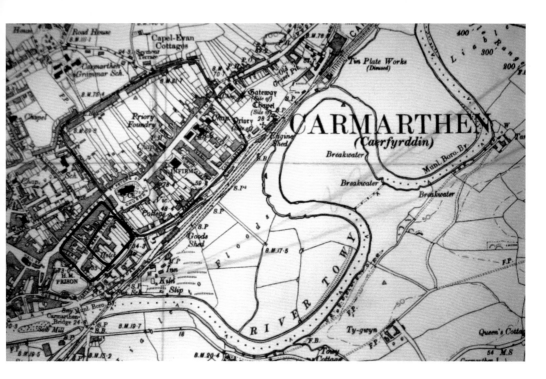

Roman Carmarthen

With reference to the above photograph, in around AD 70–74, the Demetae were granted Roman citizenship (Latin – civitas status) and a capital called Moridunum Demetarum was built for them by the Romans at British Caerfyrddin, modern Carmarthen (the rhombic area outlined in red on the map). At the same time, the Romans founded a fort to the south-west outside the town walls (the playing-card shape outlined in blue on the map). The fort appears to have been abandoned between around AD 193 and AD 217 only to be reoccupied again at a later date. By AD 382, Roman authority in the west began to fade away quickly and after the death of usurper Magnus Maximus, the area appears to have evolved into a region called Demetia. The Romans left Britannia for good between AD 409–410. The two bottom photographs show respectively the Roman altar located in the porch of St Peter's church and Roman stones on display in Carmarthen Museum.

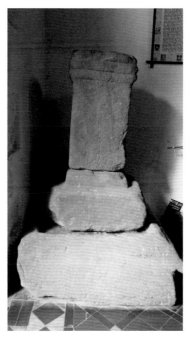

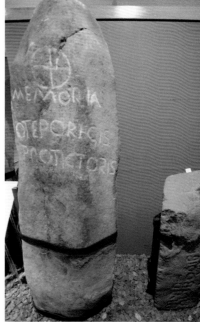

9

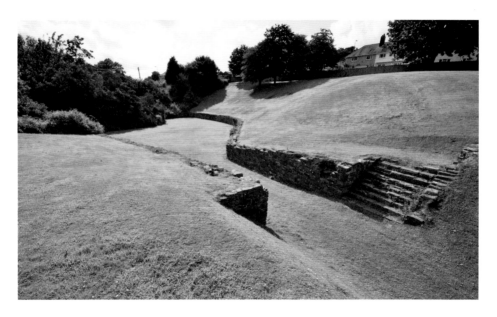

The Roman Amphitheatre

As a town, perhaps Carmarthen is unique in being able to boast that it has one of the oldest theatres in the country. The Roman amphitheatre (*amphitheatrum* in Latin) located to the north-east of the Roman town (indicated by the green elliptical circle on the map of page 9) was probably erected soon after AD 74. It is one of only three amphitheatres remaining in Wales with the others being located at Caerleon and Tomen-y-Mur ('Mound in the walls'), North Wales. The site was excavated in 1968. The arena (*harena, stadium, theatrum*) itself is 150 x 90 feet and the seating area (*cavea*) measures 300 x 219 feet. The two photographs, taken on 7 July 2015, show the entrance into the arena (top) and the seating area overlooking the arena (bottom). The inset illustrates how the whole amphitheatre, with its tiers of seats rising around the arena, would have been enclosed within a curtain wall – like a cage (*cavea).*

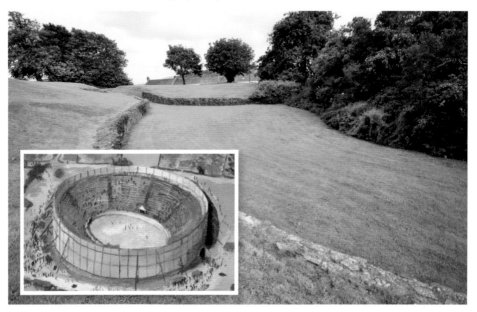

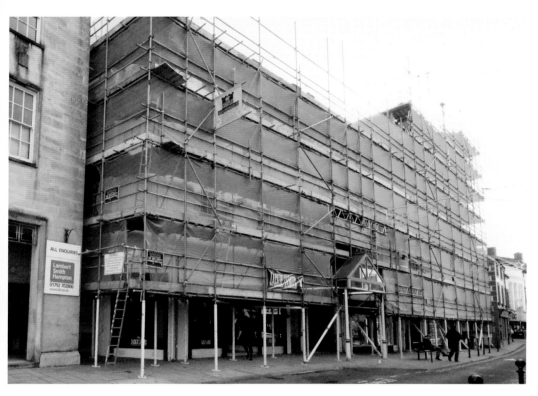

The Lyric Theatre, King Street

It is likely that the Roman amphitheatre would have been used for sports and gladiatorial displays as well as for theatrical tragedy and comedy plays. However, except for the travelling or strolling players of medieval and Norman times, it would be centuries before the theatre came to Carmarthen again. The first record of a Fit Up Company visiting Carmarthen is for the period 1734–41 when the Morrison's Company of six strolling players headed by Charles and Mary Morrison visited the town as part of a tour and performed at a local inn. Eventually, and after many years, permanent theatres were built in Carmarthen. The Lyric Theatre as we know it today, and as shown under shrouds in the two photographs, was originally the town house of the Scurlock family and was where Richard Steele, founder of *The Spectator,* died in 1729. The Lyric started life in 1854 as the Assembly Rooms. It became the Lyric Cinema in 1918 and survived until 1935 when it was closed, demolished

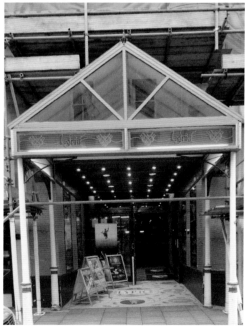

and replaced with a new modern Art Deco building to seat 1,000. It opened again the following year as the new Lyric Cinema, but fate dictated that it was to close again after a long run in 1983. Reopened again by volunteers as the Lyric Theatre, it has gone through a number refurbishment programs ever since to survive as the largest cinema auditorium in Wales.

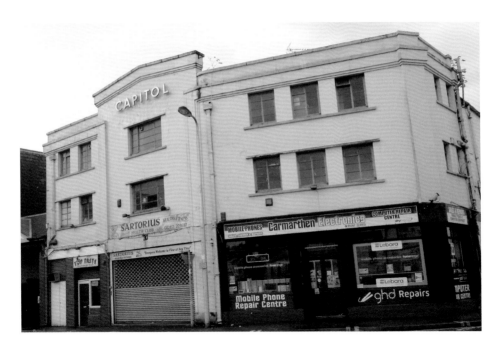

Capitol, Apollo and Vue Cinemas

The top picture shows the Capitol Cinema on the corner of Barn Road and Orchard Street. It was opened in 1929 as a lavish cinema with 1,000 seats and all the latest up-to-date equipment, offering comfort and luxury for the audience. It was used for the occasional live show and concert up to the 1960s, but is now closed and used as shops. The Apollo Cinema (bottom photograph taken on 2 October 2015), was opened on 30 April 2010 as the first 'all digital' purpose-built cinema in Wales. All six screens are equipped with digital projectors and are capable of showing 3D films. Seating capacities in the six auditoriums are 334, 208, 104, 104, 95 and 67. The venue was taken over in January 2013 and renamed the Vue Cinema.

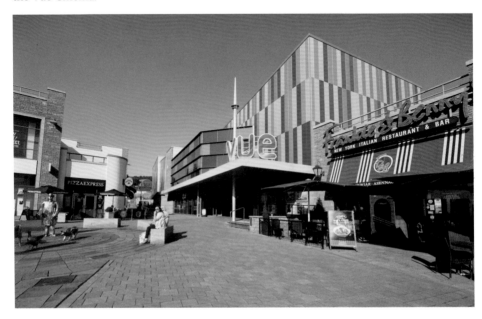

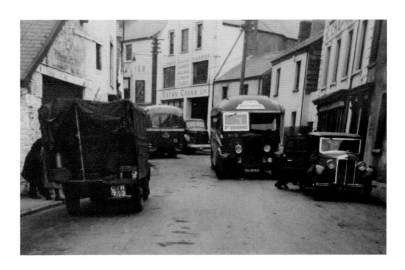

Vint's Electric Palace/Empire Theatre, Blue Street

Captured in the late 1940s or early 1950s, the top picture shows a very busy and congested Blue Street with two Western Welsh single-deck half-cab buses trying to navigate their way through the busy thoroughfare past Oscar Chess' garage tucked away up in the top corner. The latter was not always a garage. Before it became a garage in 1938, it was a theatre. Designed by Ernest Collier, it opened on 1 April 1912 as Vint's Electric Palace. The Palace, with a seating capacity for 600 people, had 'modern' electrical heating, ventilation and plumbing. As well as being a cinema, Vint's Palace was also a theatre for the staging of plays and variety performances. Leon Vint was an entrepreneur and as well as owning the Carmarthen Palace, he controlled a number of other Palace Theatres throughout the country. His portrait is shown in the inset by kind permission of the Nuneaton Local History Group. However, by February 1914 Vint had overstretched himself financially and had to sell up. The Palace closed only to reopen one week later as the Empire Theatre. The latter theatre had its own orchestra and put on a wide range of variety acts and 'pictures'. Eventually, its popularity waned and it was sold to Oscar Chess in 1938 for use as a garage. As shown below, the building houses two shops at street level and a restaurant on the first floor.

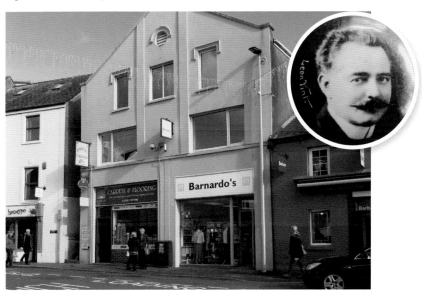

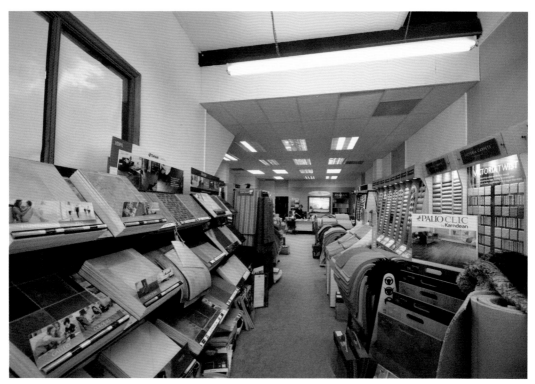

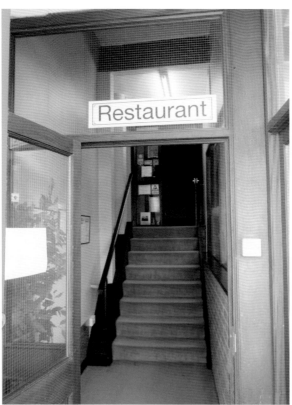

Vint's Electric Palace/Empire Theatre, Blue Street

Oscar Chess' garage has long gone and Barnado's has taken over one part of what was originally the ground floor of Vint's Picture Palace. The other part has been converted into a carpet showroom. Apparently, the garage vehicle service pit still exists underneath the floor coverings in this area. On the left of the carpet showroom, two flights of very steep stairs take you up to Pantri Blakeman. The restaurant, run by sisters Moyra and Carol Blakeman, specialises in home-cooked Welsh cuisine, which is a real treat.

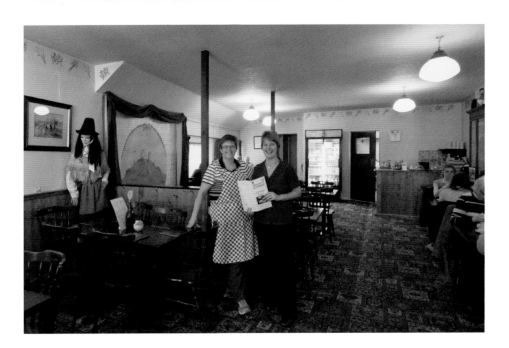

Pantri Blakeman, Blue Street

As illustrated in the top photograph, taken in October 2015, Pantri Blakeman occupies the first floor of what was once Vint's Picture Palace. There is also another floor above. The same picture shows sisters Carol (left) and Moyra holding a copy of the menu that attracts so many customers to the restaurant. In 2011, Pantri Blakeman was awarded five stars for hygiene by the Foods Standards Agency. The restaurant also raises a lot of money for charity and has the honour of having had a musical item written on its premises; 'Moyra' was presented by its author Dorothy Jones at the 2013 Welsh National Eisteddfod.

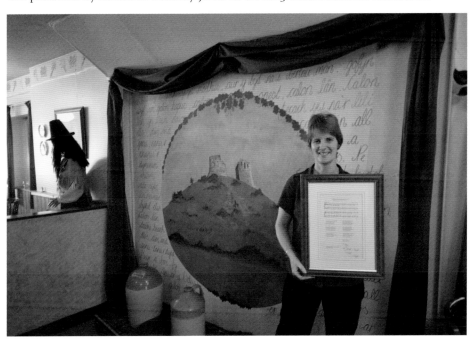

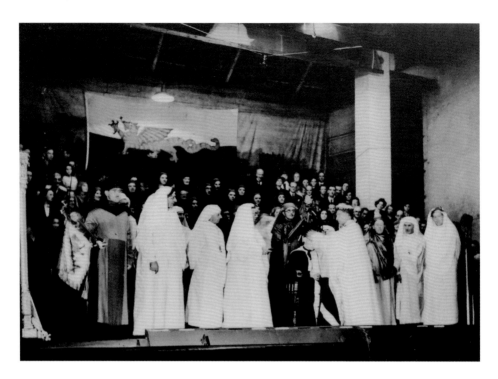

Eisteddfod Genedlaethol Cymru/National Eisteddfod of Wales

The two photographs, both from the Carmarthen Museum Photograph Archives, capture scenes from the National Eisteddfod, the Gorsedd, held in Carmarthen Park in 1911. The inset profile is of Edward Williams (1747–1826) who is better known by his bardic name, Iolo Morganwg (Iolo of Glamorgan). In his day, Iolo was an influential Welsh antiquarian, poet and collector who, after his death, was considered to be a literary forger! Nevertheless, Iolo has had a lasting impact on Welsh culture, notably his founding of the Gorsedd, which he established in 1792 on Primrose Hill in London. But it was in the Ivy Bush Hotel (now a car park) that he held his first Eisteddfod Gorsedd at the 1819 Carmarthen Eisteddfod.

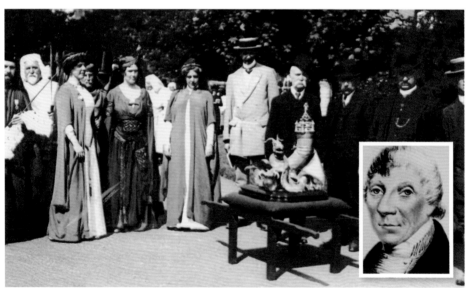

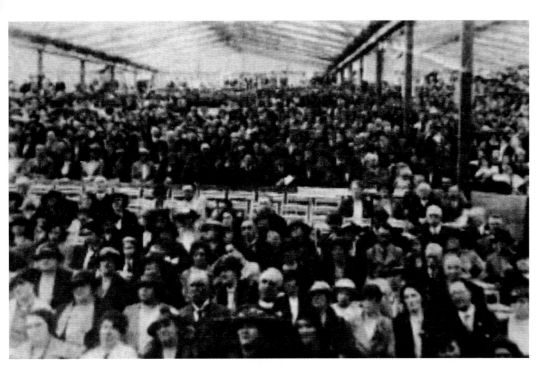

Eisteddfod Genedlaethol Cymru/National Eisteddfod of Wales
More photographs of the Eisteddfod held in Carmarthen in 1911, this time from the records of the Carmarthen Town Council. The top picture was taken in the Eisteddfod Pavilion of 1911 while the bottom image is a scene from the Gorsedd Ceremony of 1973.

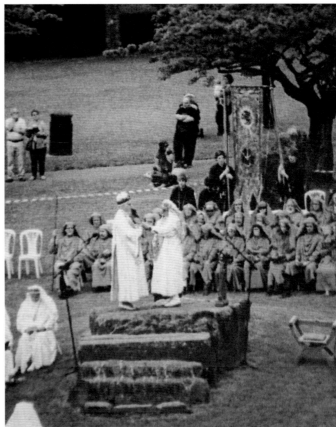

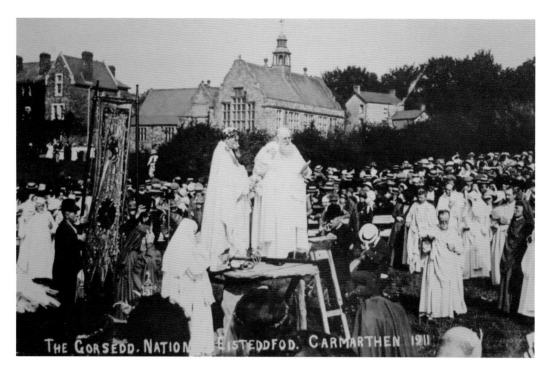

Eisteddfod Genedlaethol Cymru/National Eisteddfod of Wales

Then and now views of the Eisteddfod have been recorded in the two photographs on this page. The top picture is from the Eisteddfod proclamation ceremony in Carmarthen Park, 1911 (Carmarthen Museum), while in the lower image, local photographer Ken Davies has captured the same event in the 1973 Eisteddfod, also held at Carmarthen Park.

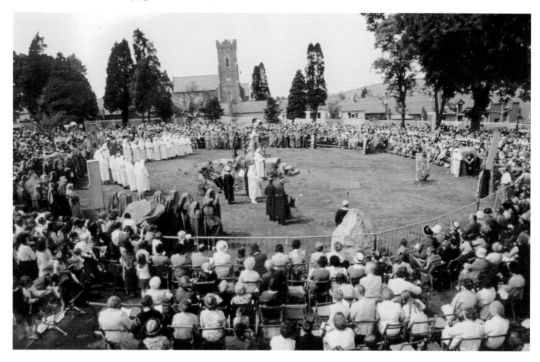

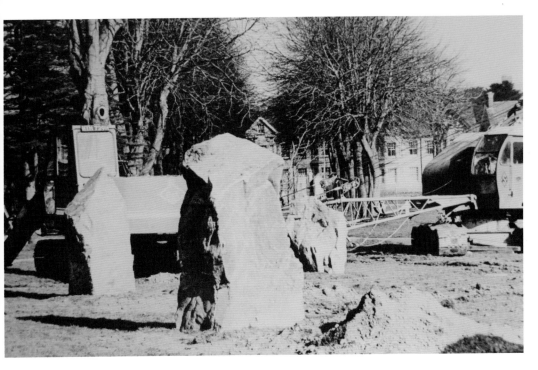

Gorsedd Circle

As shown in the top photograph from the Carmarthen Museum Archives, the Gorsedd Circle was erected in 1973 ready for the proclamation ceremony of the 1974 Eisteddfod Bro Myrddin. The lower picture of the Gorsedd Circle was taken on 30 June 2015.

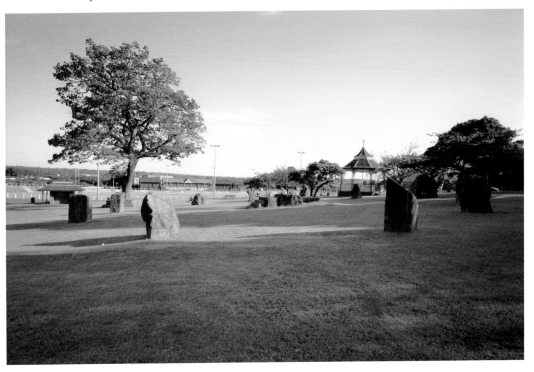

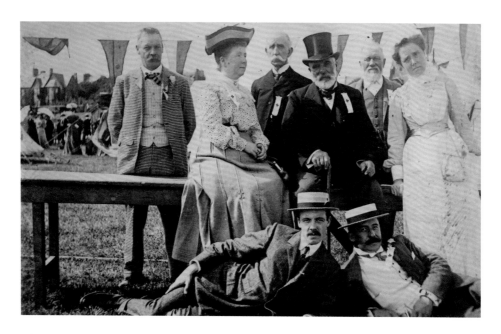

The Carmarthen Park

Carmarthen Park was opened on Easter Monday at a grand opening ceremony in 1900. The top photograph was probably taken on this occasion. It was estimated that 7-8,000 people attended the official opening by Sir James Drummond, Bart of Edwinsford and Lord Lieutenant of the county. An Enabling Act of Parliament dated 10 November 1897 referred to a proposed application for improvements to Carmarthen which involved the creation of a new park on a 12-acre site off Morfa Lane. The land, owned by the Ecclesiastical Commissioners, was to be turned into recreation grounds covering all manner of sports and like activities. The park, designed by the borough surveyor Fred J. Finglah, was to include a velodrome (as shown in the lower photograph) and the philosophy at the time was that 'They must keep ahead of the times and have a cement track.'

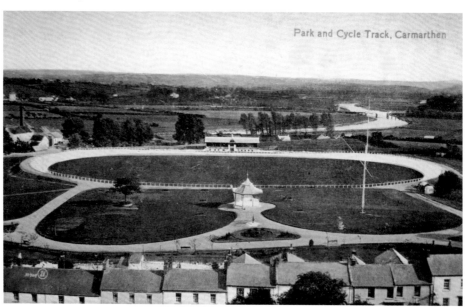

Park and Cycle Track, Carmarthen

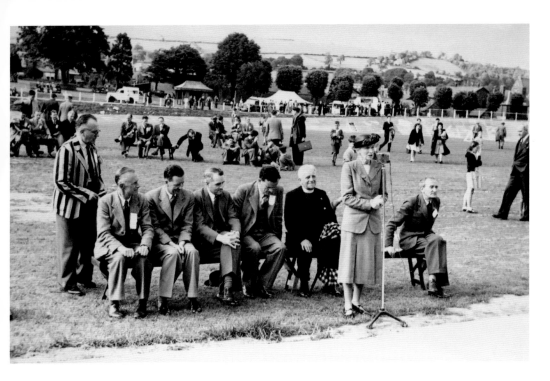

The Carmarthen Park

As specified in the 1897 bill, Carmarthen Park does embrace many different sports and other activities. The top image is of Margaret Childe-Villiers, then Lady Dynevor, opening the County Sports sometime in the 1950s, while use of the park for soccer is illustrated in the bottom photograph.

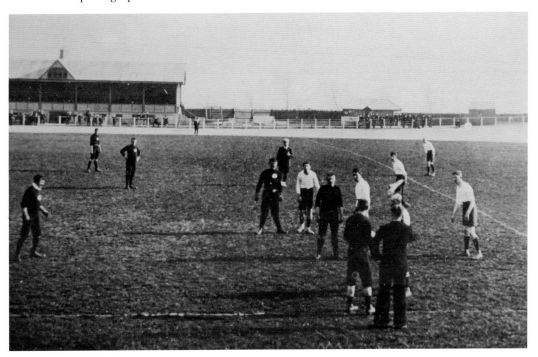

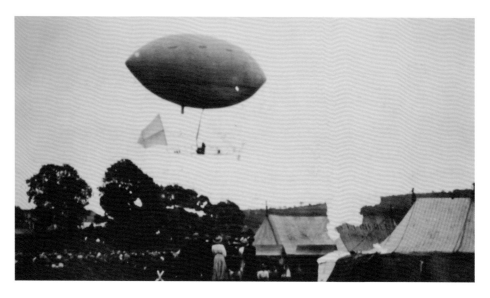

Carmarthen Park

Following the opening of the park, many spectacular events were put on to entertain the crowds that flocked in to see them. The top photograph (Carmarthen Museum) records the first ascent of an airship in Wales, which took place at the park in 1908. Eight years earlier, the famous Spencer Brothers of Highbury, London, Balloon Manufacturers, had brought a hot-air balloon to Carmarthen to demonstrate at the park. Apparently thousands turned out to watch this unique event, which was due to start at 4.00 p.m. but was delayed until a rip in the silk fabric had been repaired by two local women. When the 80-foot balloon did eventually take off at 7.00 p.m., with its passengers suspended below it in a bamboo basket, most of the spectators had gone. The lower photograph from the J. F. Lloyd Collection at the Carmarthen Museum shows the 'Rossi and Spinelli music machine' that would have entertained at the park during the period 1900–05. These traditional hand-cranked musical instruments of the Italian immigrants to this country from Bardi in Northern Italy were also called 'barrel/roller organs' or 'hurdy gurdies'.

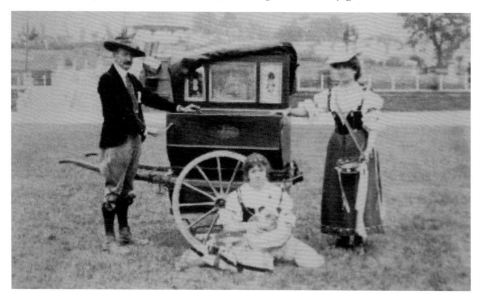

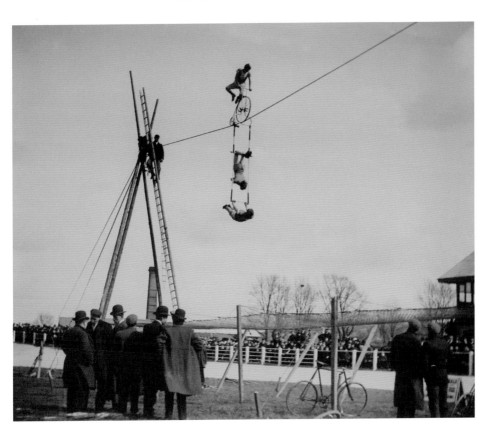

Carmarthen Park

Trick cyclists and aerobatic cycle acts were great attractions at the park in the early days of the 1900s, as shown in the top photograph from the Carmarthen Museum Archives. There had been great support for cycle racing in Carmarthen since around 1877 when the races actually took place in the town. The velodrome with its concrete circuit proved to be a magnet for world champion cyclists and many competitions were held here. The bottom photograph from the J. F. D. Lloyd Collection at the Carmarthen Museum shows such a competitor in around 1900.

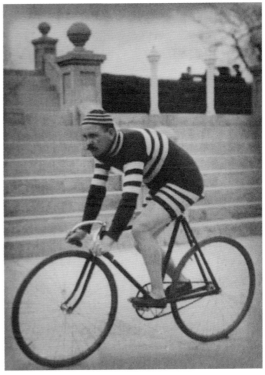

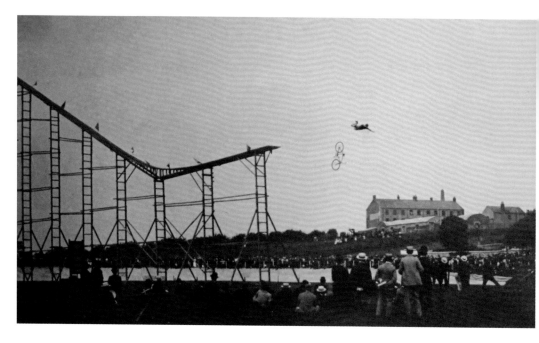

Carmarthen Park

World-class entertainers were invited to perform in the park. One of these was the American daredevil aerial cyclist Max Schreyer, advertised as 'the greatest sensation on earth'. Preserved for all time in the Carmarthen Museum, is the top photograph taken of Max in 1905 doing his spectacular cyclist act at the Park. On his bicycle, Max would ride off a 103-foot-high chute, spring from the saddle, dive 100 feet through the air and land head first in a tank of water. Phew! He also performed throughout the world in locations including London, Paris and New York. However, those days are long gone and today's performers, such as the Circus Zyair, are much more down to earth.

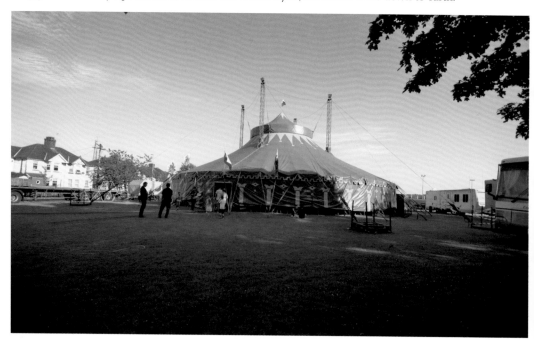

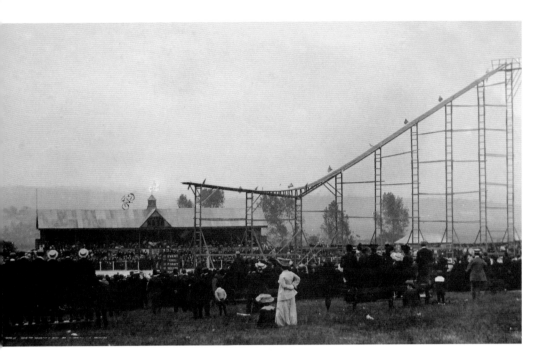

Carmarthen Park

Another photograph of daredevil Max Schreyer from the opposite direction, captured as he leaps of his bicycle and straightens out into his headlong dive into the water tank 100 feet below. The lower photograph was taken in June 2015 when the Circus Zyair was doing its 2015 tour of the UK. These performers present a colourful and action-packed hour-and-a-half performance with high-energy acts from all over the world. Perhaps not so down to earth after all?

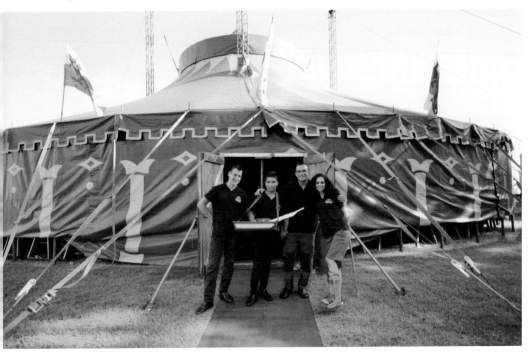

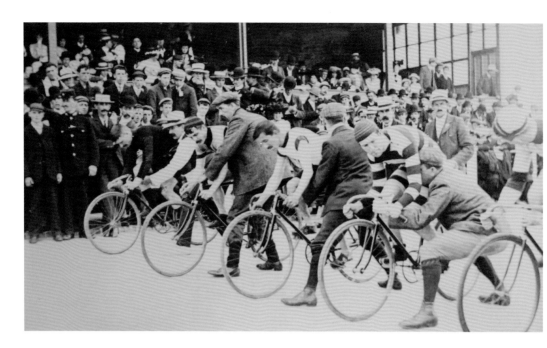

Carmarthen Park – The Velodrome

Centre stage of the park is the velodrome with its concrete circuit measuring 1,330 feet (405.38 metres) long. It was officially opened on Easter Monday in 1900 and has been in continuous use ever since. As such, it is reputed to be the oldest outdoor concrete velodrome in continuous use in the world. It was on this circuit that the concept of 'pacing' a cyclist behind a motorcyclist to attain higher speeds is reputed to having been first introduced. The two photographs compare the early exciting days of cycle racing in the velodrome in the early 1900s with the leisurely training of young cyclists at the velodrome today.

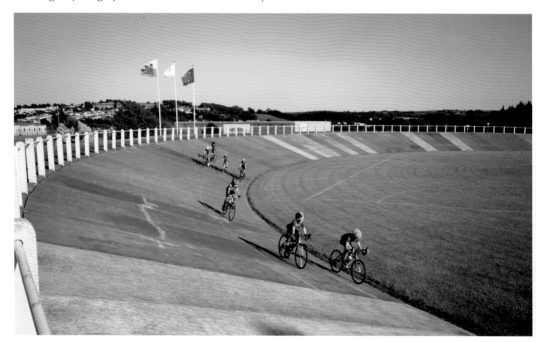

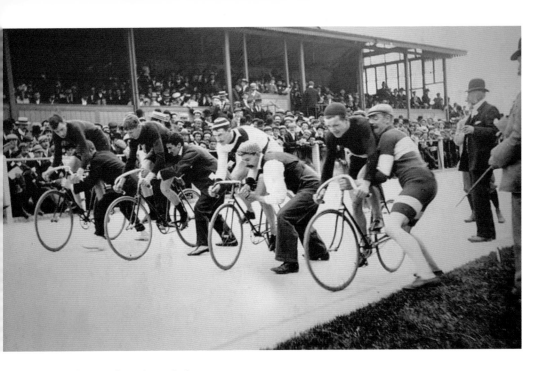

Carmarthen Park – The Velodrome

The top photograph (provided by the Carmarthen Town Council) not only captures the excitement and enthusiasm of the cyclists and spectators in the early days of racing at the velodrome, but also the fascinating stances of the 'cycle pushers' who were there, no doubt, to give their respective cyclist a good kick-start to the race. Today, the velodrome is as splendid as ever, having received a number of upgrades and developments over the years with current plans in hand to turn it into a Cycling Hub.

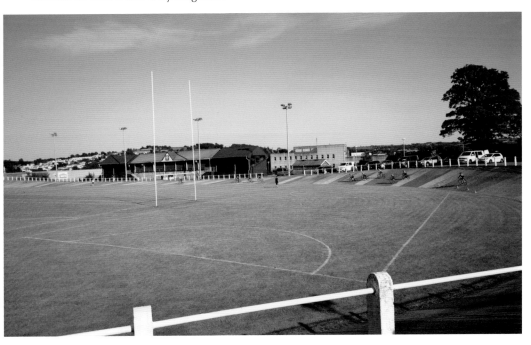

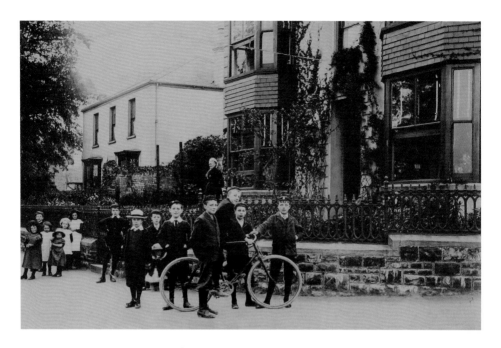

Transport

The excitement of the velodrome would have created an interest and enthusiasm with every boy to own a bicycle. We have a young lad here in this photograph taken on The Parade during the early 1900s, proudly showing off his prized possession to his school pals and friends outside 'Rydal Mount', the Esplanade, around 1910. The lady in the garden is probably Mrs. Pugh Evans, widow of a Vicar of St Peter's. The boys are wearing what look like Grammar School cap badges. At this time in the early 1900s, the motor car had yet to make its mark. Invented in 1886 by Karl Benz, the general mode of transport in the early 1900s was still the horse and carriage, as shown in the lower image.

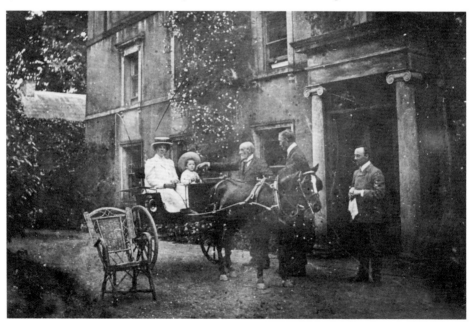

Transport

When the motor car did finally arrive, it was usually only the privilege of the wealthy as few others could afford one. It was not until after the end of the Second World War that motor cars really started to became available to everyone, with sales slowly escalating, leading to the phenomenal number of vehicles on today's roads. The top photograph is of an early Morgan 4/4 of vintage 1935–39 standing outside the premises of W. Edwards & Co. of what looks to be a motorcycle shop. Note the old (and probably hand-operated) Shell petrol pump on the left of the picture. Harry Morgan, the inventor of the Morgan 3-Wheeler Runabout, first introduced in November 1910, can be regarded as the man who first introduced motoring for the masses. Still going strong, the bottom photograph shows a line-up of modern Morgan cars in front of the Felinfoel Restaurant Car Suite at the Gwili Railway.

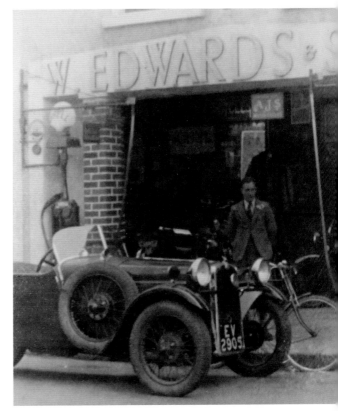

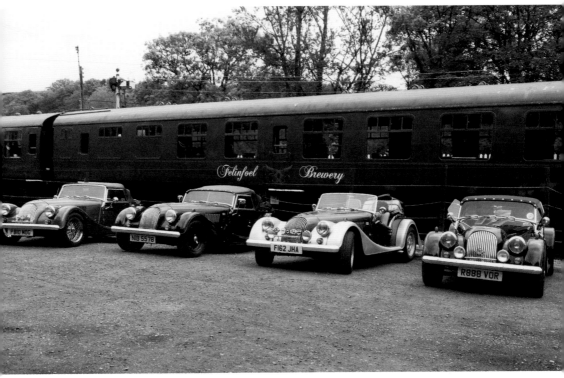

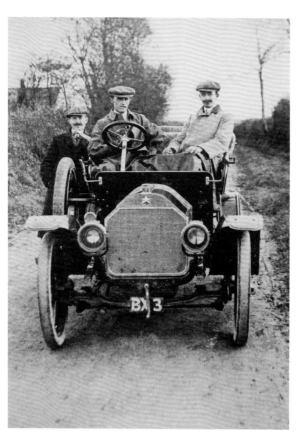

Transport

Two pictures of vehicles on the road in Carmarthen in the early days of motoring. The top image is possibly of an early Ariel-Simplex while the second picture, taken in Lammas Street, is probably of the same make and chassis but with a 'delivery van' body. The sign work on the side of this van proudly announces that it belongs to 'Evan Morris & Sons' of the 'Top Hat Carmarthen', the agents for 'N & C Nicholson Rain Coats' and that they do a 'Country Order Service'. The vehicle also has a Stepney spare wheel. The latter was invented by Thomas Morris Davies of Llanelli in 1904. At that time, early motor cars were made without spare wheels, so a puncture was an event dreaded by all drivers. Davies' brilliant idea was to make a spoke-less wheel rim fitted with an inflated tyre that could be bolted onto the wheel with the puncture. His success lasted until 1922 when car manufacturers began to provide spare wheels with all new cars.

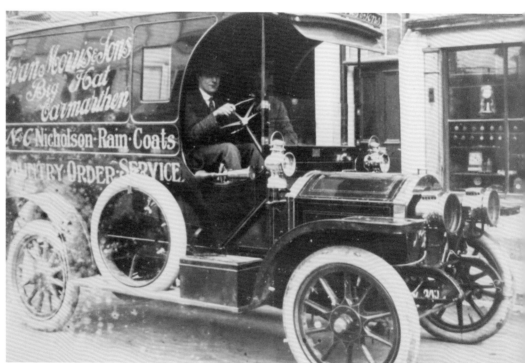

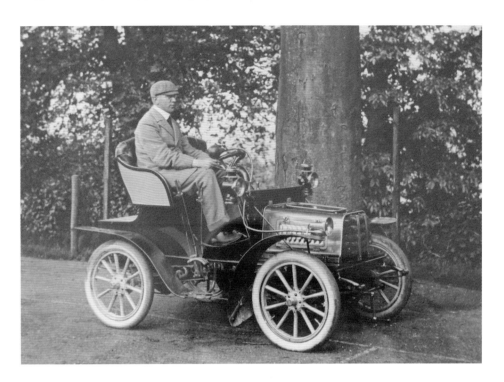

Transport

Two more cars of the early days of motoring in Carmarthen. Judging by their distinctive radiator grills, they both could be 1904 Sunbeams. Note the heavy raincoat worn by the driver of the car in the lower photograph. This was a necessity as when travelling in these vehicles drivers and passengers were exposed to the elements.

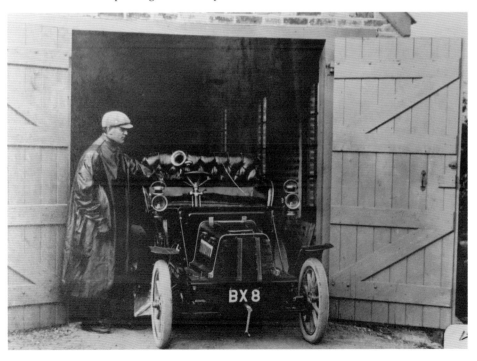

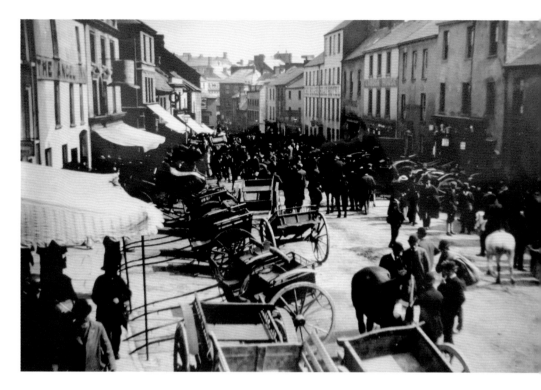

Transport

The hustle and bustle of the Horse Fair in Lammas Street around the early 1900s with a predominance of horse-drawn buggies. Note the bowler-hatted farmers in the foreground, possibly carrying on some horse trading. A far cry from the modern bus terminal alongside the Greyfriars Shopping Centre bordering on Blue Street, shown in the bottom photograph taken on 7 November 2015.

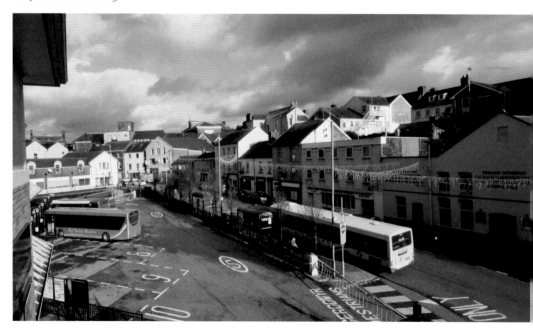

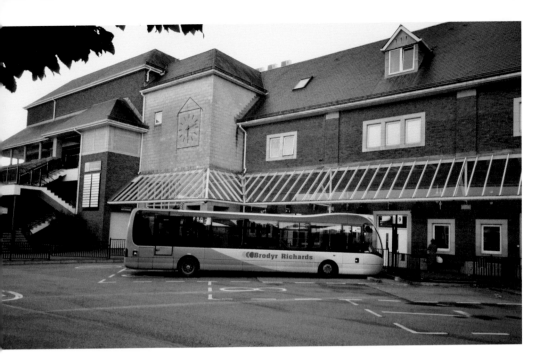

Transport

Another view of the Horse Fair in Lammas Street, this time taken in the 1940s when the motor car, lorry and bus have convincingly taken over from the horse-drawn traps and buggies of the early 1900s. Note the single-decker half-cab bus on the right of the picture which appears to be a throwback to the char-a-banc days and compare it with the photograph taken of the modern bus taken in the bus station on 22 September 2015.

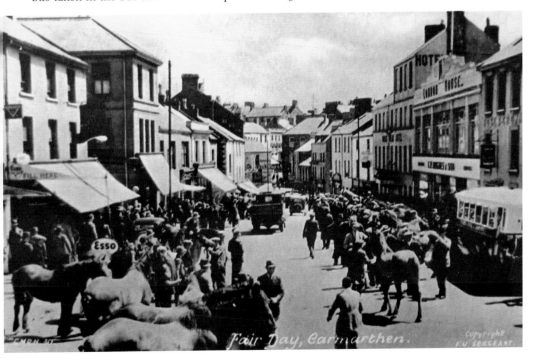

Fair Day, Carmarthen.

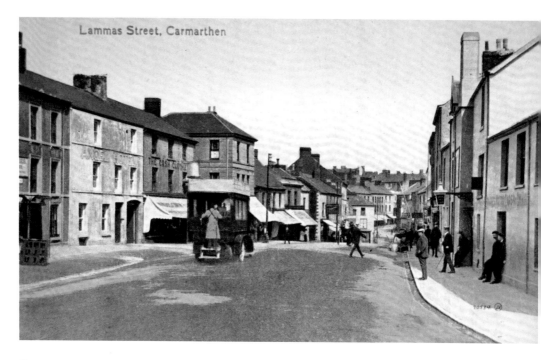

Lammas Street, Carmarthen

Transport

Lammas Street in the 1900s with what looks like an motor-driven omnibus in front of the Angel Hotel and the premises of Evan Morris & Sons, Top Hat, proudly advertising to be 'Cash Clothiers'. Note the fare collecting conductor riding on the back steps of the omnibus. Compare this early form of public transport with Brodyr Richards' modern omnibus leaving the railway station yard in October 2010.

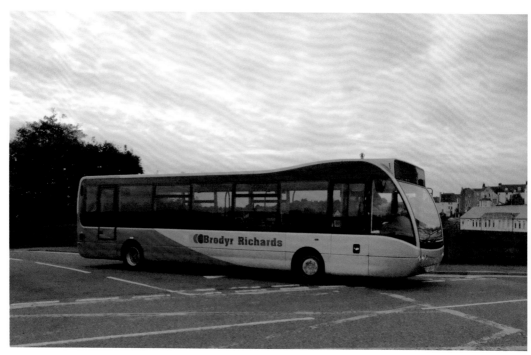

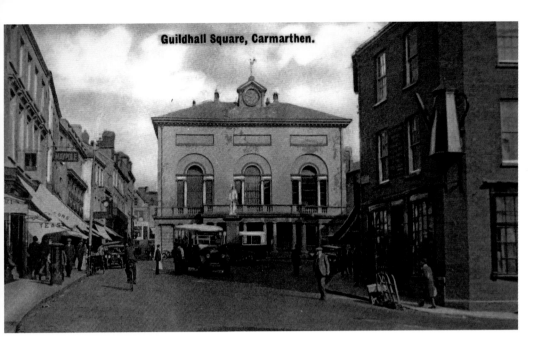

Guildhall Square, Carmarthen.

Transport

Public transport char-a-bancs in Guildhall Square in the late 1920s/early 1930s. Note the giant black-coloured metal coffee pot mounted on the corner of the building on the right-hand side of the photograph. This was once used to advertise Miss Puddiscome's grocery shop. The grocery shop has long gone; the premises now house a savings bank, but the coffee pot is still there, as shown in the inset photograph. As with a number of other buses in the fleet, the bus in the lower photograph has been sprayed in the distinctive colours of Thomas Bros by the First Choice Bus Co. as part of the celebrations for their first 100 years of service, 1914–2014.

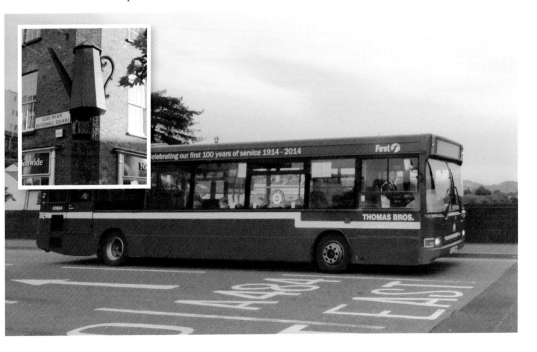

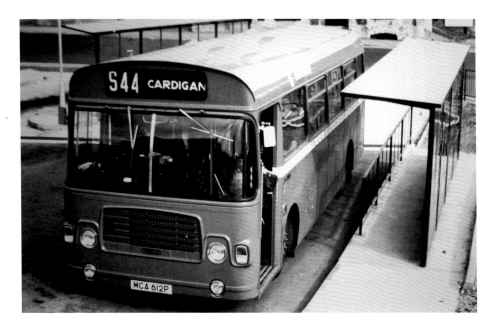

Transport

The top photograph shows Crosville bus MCA 612P on the Cardigan Route at Carmarthen on 23 July 1976 while the lower photograph is of a TrawsCymru coach as it leaves Carmarthen Railway Station on 7 July 2015. TrawsCymru, the long-distance bus service for Wales, is an important part of the integrated public transport network in Wales. The service is funded by the Welsh government, with the buses providing vital public transport for many communities across the principality as well as giving visitors an accessible, affordable and environmentally friendly option for exploring the scenic beauty of the country. Currently there are six interlinking routes operated by the TrawsCymru service.

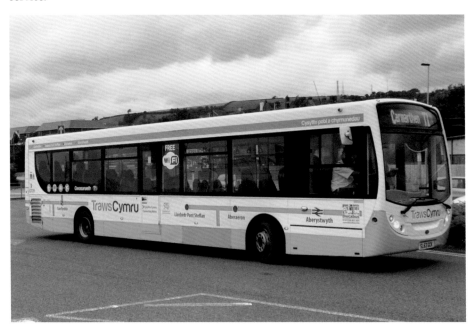

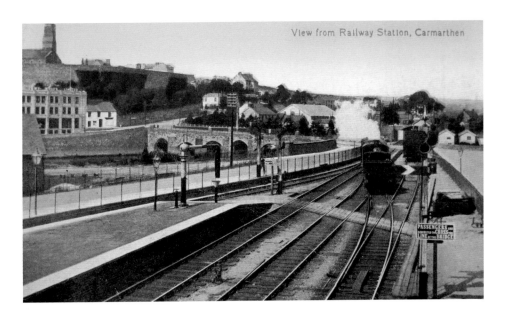

The Railways

The railway came to Carmarthen as a broad-gauge line in 1852 courtesy of Isambard Kingdom Brunel, the Great Western Railway engineer, and formed an initial part of the South Wales Railway extending west to Neyland (New Milford) in Pembrokeshire as part of the rapidly expanding railway network of the era. The main east-west line looped into Carmarthen as a triangular spur while the eventual branch line links north to the coal mines, Llandeilo and Aberystwyth, carried straight on through. The top postcard view (Carmarthen Museum) looking northwards would have been taken before 1936 when the old road bridge across the river was demolished. As shown in the lower 'end-of-the-line' photograph taken on 2 October 2015, Carmarthen station is now a terminus for the main London-Fishguard east-west line with only two of its original five platforms remaining. The first closures of the branch lines north, were felt as early as 1951 with final closure to goods traffic taking place in 1973.

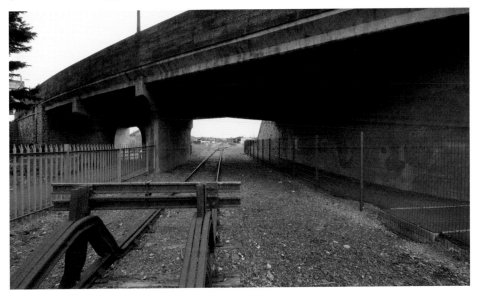

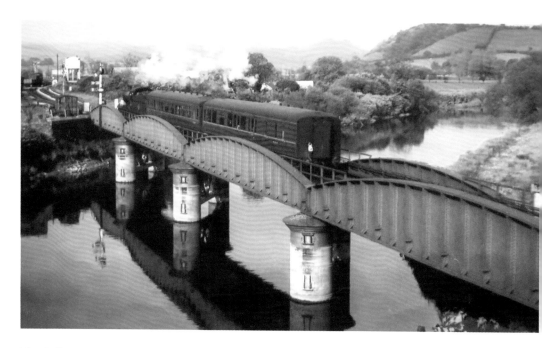

The Railways

The top picture shows a passenger train crossing the Towy River en route from Carmarthen to Aberystwyth. The photograph would have been taken before February 1965 when the line was closed to passenger traffic. The single-track iron girder railway bridge, built in 1858, was subsequently removed during 1983 and a new bridge constructed further upstream in 1999 to carry the eastern bypass road, the A40(T), from Pen-sarn, south of Carmarthen to Abergwili, north-east of the town. The latter is as shown in the lower photograph, taken in October 2015, and once across the river, this new road mainly follows the line of the old railway track to what was Abergwili Junction

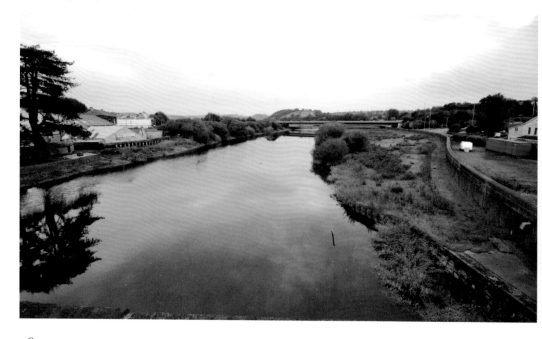

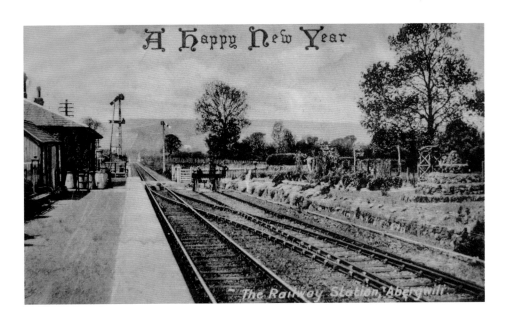

The Railway Station, Abergwili

The Railways

The station at Abergwili village, as reproduced in the top image from a postcard carrying a 'Happy New Year' message, was closed in September 1963 when the Llandeilo branch line went under. The extension of the eastern bypass, referred to on page 38, is built on the track of the old line that passed through the station and met with and joined the 'main' line to Aberystwyth at Abergwili Junction. The Aberystwyth line, which finally closed to freight traffic in 1973, is now owned from Abergwili Junction northwards by the Gwili Steam Railway. The latter runs preserved trains up the line from Bronwydd Arms to Danycoed, near to Cynwyl Elfed. The track has also been extended south from Bronwydd Arms as far as Abergwili Junction, which as shown in the lower photograph, is still under construction. The inset photograph shows the author posing at the 'end-of-line' buffers of this latest extension.

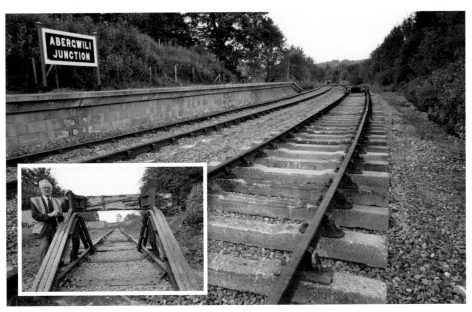

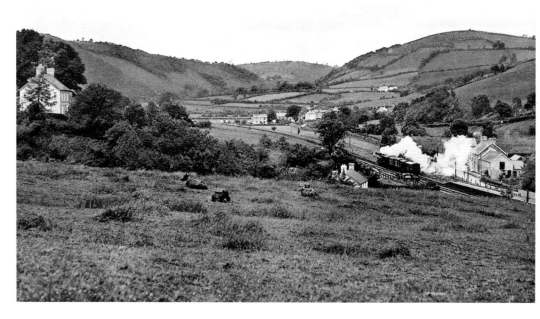

The Gwili Railway

The top view is of a small freight train progressing slowly north out of the Bronwydd Arms Station in around 1952. In the lower photograph, the author has captured Felinfoel Brewery's locomotive, *The Welsh Guardsman* steaming away under full power, hauling an excursion train from the same station during the Gwili Steam Railway's Gala Day on 10 October 2015.

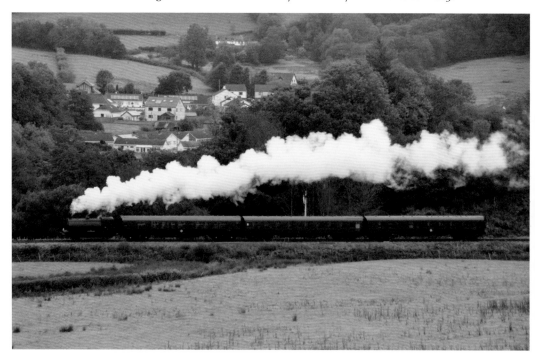

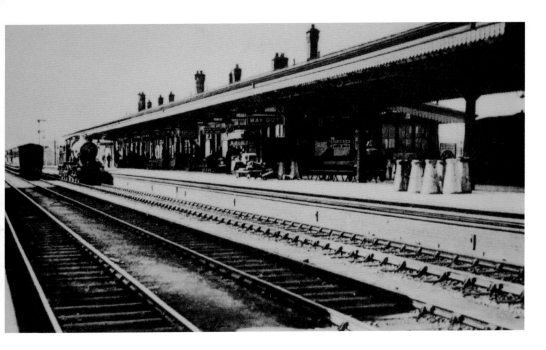

The Railways – Carmarthen Station

Two views of Carmarthen Station are illustrated on this page. The top photograph, from the Carmarthen Museum Archives, was probably taken in the 1950s looking south along what was Platform No. 2 (now No. 1) when the station still had three sets of railway lines running between the two platforms. Note the old-fashioned milk churns standing on the end of the platform. The more recent photograph was taken in July 2015 along the same direction with Platform No. 2 (was No. 3) on the left and the main active platform, Platform No. 1, on the right. The remains of the ballasted centre track are still visible.

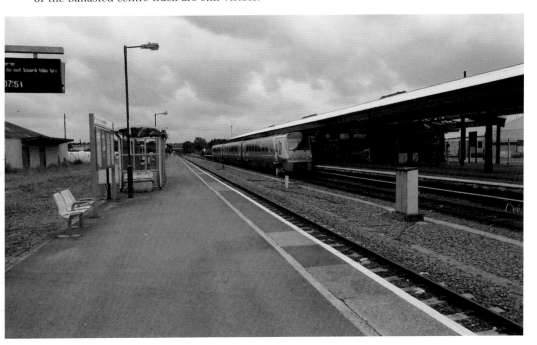

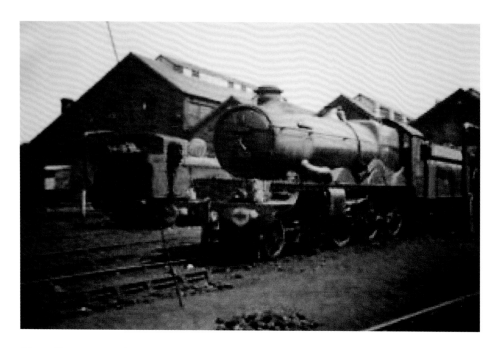

The Railways – Motive Power

Steam finished on the Western Region at the beginning of 1966. The top photograph of Castle Class No. 4076 *Carmarthen Castle* was taken at Carmarthen Station in 1961. *Carmarthen Castle* was built at Swindon in February 1924 as one of a class of over 200 express engines used all over the GWR network. After thirty-nine years' service, it was withdrawn from use in February 1963. The inset shows a photograph of the *Carmarthen Castle* nameplate on display in the foyer of the Carmarthen Town Council offices, while the bottom picture is of a modern Arriva DMU (Diesel Multiple Unit) train at Carmarthen Station on 7 July 2015.

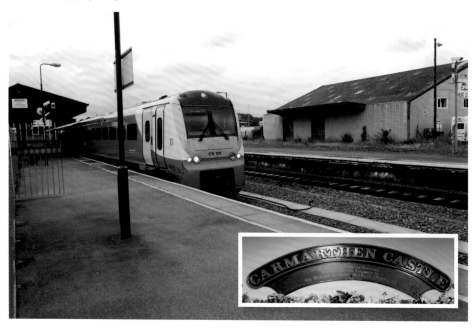

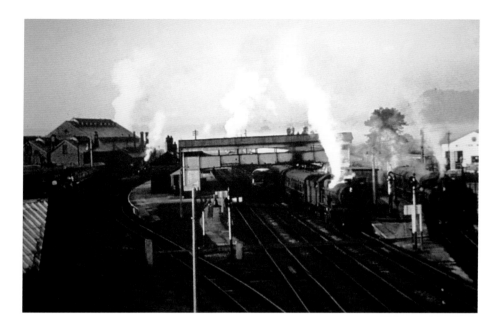

Railways – Carmarthen Station

A busy Carmarthen Station is pictured in the top photograph which brings all five platforms together, with the engine sheds on the left. The 'up-stopper' standing at Platform No.2 is pulled by Castle Class No. 4076 'Carmarthen Castle'. What a contrast to the lower picture taken from the same standpoint on 7 July 2015, which shows a much quieter Carmarthen Station. Since 1973, the latter station has been left as a terminus at the end of a short spur from the main line at which all trains have to reverse before continuing their journeys. Not so much of a problem for modern DMUs (Diesel Multiple Units) which have driver cabs at each end, but which led to the need for a run around of steam locomotive-hauled trains, which were regularly used until the mid-1980s.

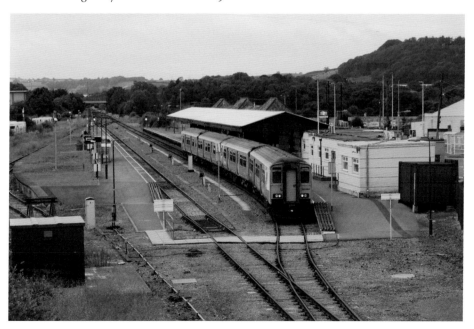

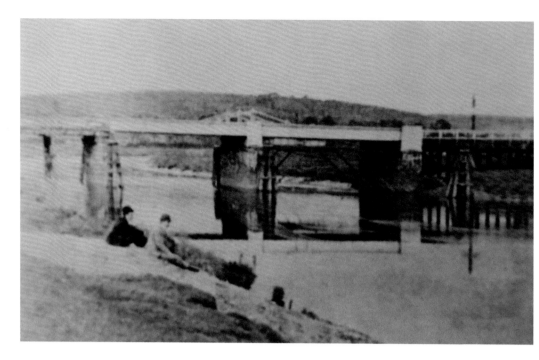

The Railways – The White Bridge at Llangunnor

Trains to and from the west cross over the River Towy at the western edge of Carmarthen Junction, a triangular junction around 700 meters south-west of the railway station, via a bascule bridge which carries twin-track railway lines. This bridge, the White , was built in 1908–11 by the Cleveland Bridge and Engineering Co. to replace Brunel's original opening timber bridge of 1852–53, shown in the above rather old and faded photograph. Captured in the lower photograph are railway workers typical of this early period.

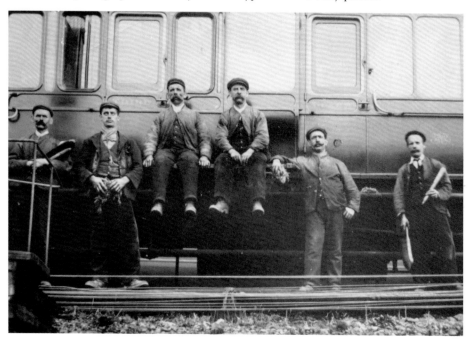

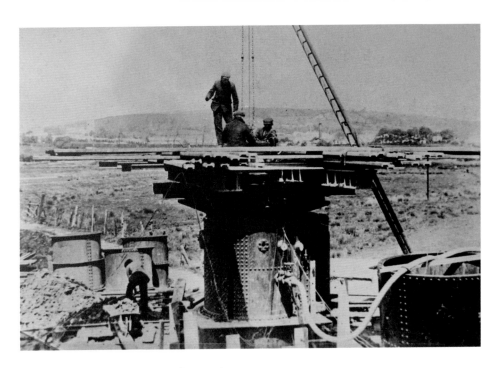

The Railways – The White Bridge at Llangunnor

Construction of the bascule bridge in 1908–11 is shown underway in the top picture while the lower image is of a drawing highlighting the details involved in the building of such a bridge. The bridge is a combination of a standard bridge with a single-span bascule section on the right (west side). *Bascule* is French for seesaw or balance and a bascule bridge is a moveable bridge section or span with a counterweight to balance the span during its upward swing to give clearance for river traffic passing below.

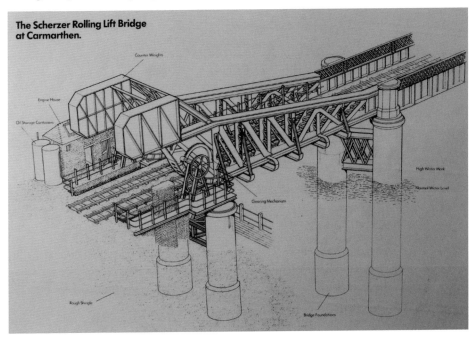

The Scherzer Rolling Lift Bridge at Carmarthen.

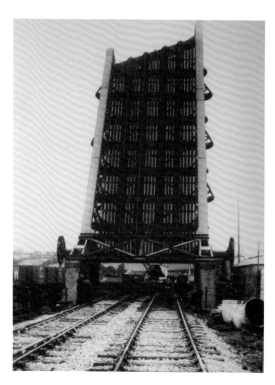

The Railways – The White Bridge at Llangunnor

In the top picture, the bascule span is shown in its raised position, possibly some time in 1911 when it was undergoing trials. The lower photograph shows the bascule bridge on 31 October 2015, still in use as a railway bridge, but the last time the bascule span was raised to allow shipping up the River Towy to reach the quays at Carmarthen was in 1950.

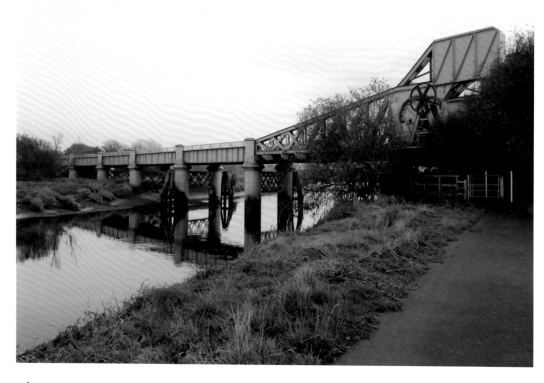

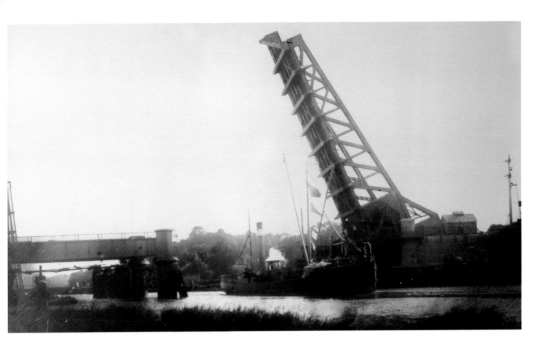

The Railways – The White Bridge, Llangunnor

The bascule bridge under construction 1908–11 is shown in the top picture. The lower close-up view of the now derelict mechanism of the bascule bridge was taken by the author early evening on 31 October 2015. Passing under the structure on the narrow footpath, bounded on one side by the silent but fast-flowing River Towy, he found it very eerie and a little bit awe-inspiring to be so close to this once very powerful mechanical engineering structure. For those who wish to view the bascule bridge and sample a similar experience, follow the public footpath from the B & Q store on the outskirts of town near Johnstown.

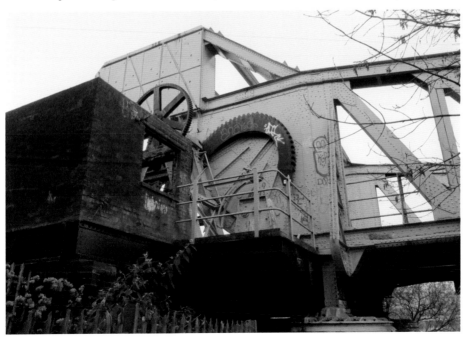

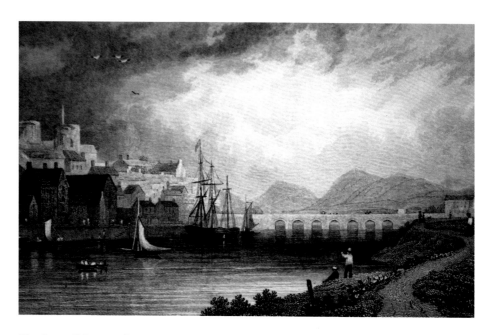

The Port of Carmarthen

Carmarthen has been a 'port' since Roman and then Norman times, when it was important to be sited on river estuaries in order to control strategic river crossings and to be supplied by sea. In the thirteenth century, ships were bringing wine to the castle garrison and the old town records of this period often refer to the importance of the river for trade. As shown in the 1830–31 engraving by Thomas Barber, quite large seagoing sailing ships were able to reach the town upstream as far as the old medieval bridge. Between 1566 and 1603, it was recorded that around fifty-eight ships carried goods into Carmarthen while a further estimated eighty-nine vessels left the port with exports for France, Ireland and Scotland. No such trade exists today, allowing road bridges like that of the A40 western bypass, shown in the lower photograph of 31 October 2015, to be built in the 1980s to circumvent both 'port' and town.

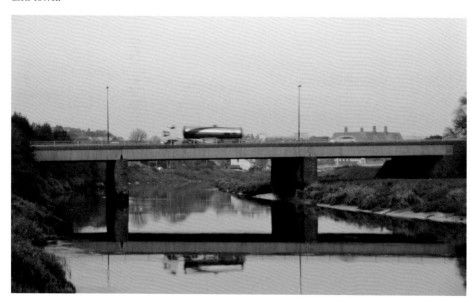

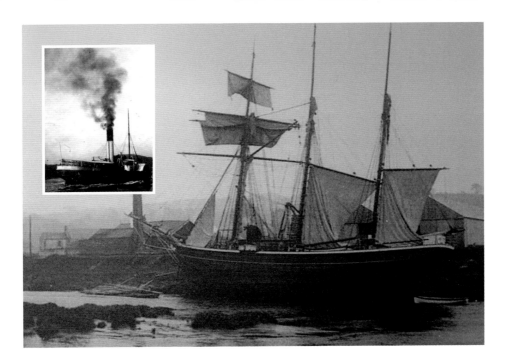

The Port of Carmarthen

The Port of Carmarthen, shown in the above picture from the Coracle Museum Collection, was photographed by John Francis Lloyd in around 1900. The ship is probably a Baltic trader bringing timber to Carmarthen. The ship was moored next to the Bulwarks' timber yard, which is on the southern bank of the river, adjacent to the railway station. The bottom photograph, taken during the River Festival held on 29 August 2015, shows the type and size of 'large' boats that one expects to see on the River Towy today. The inset photograph is of a steam tug that would have been need to manoeuvre some of the heavier sailing ships plying their trade in the port in the early twentieth century.

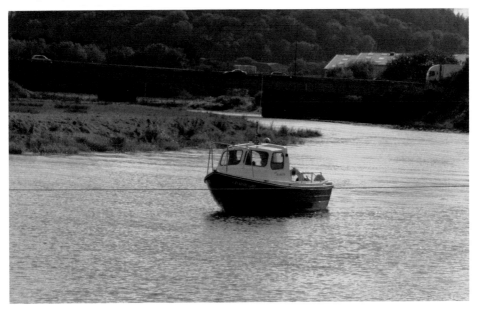

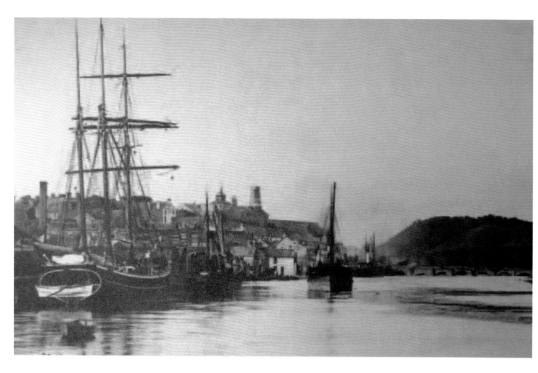

The Port of Carmarthen
Another picture from the Coracle Museum Collection showing a number of fairly large sailing ships berthed at the quay. The lower photograph has captured the arrival of the RNLI Ferryside Inflatable Inshore Lifeboat as it passes the safety marshal's boat to take up station during the Carmarthen River Festival, 29 August 2015.

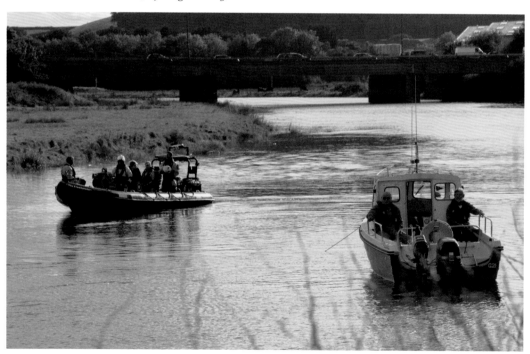

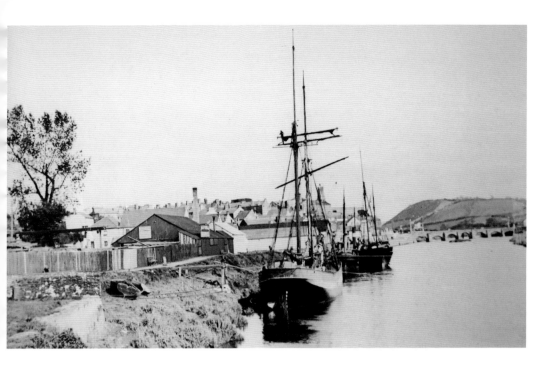

Port of Carmarthen

Yet another example of the large sailing vessels of anything up to and including 200 tons, this time from the Carmarthen Museum Archives, that were able to navigate up the River Towy from the sea. Those times have long gone and Carmarthen is no longer a port. Today, the River Towy is mainly used for recreational craft such as the kayaks shown in the lower picture giving a demonstration during the 2015 Carmarthen River Festival.

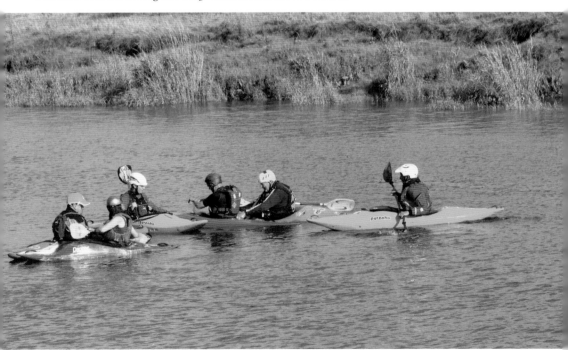

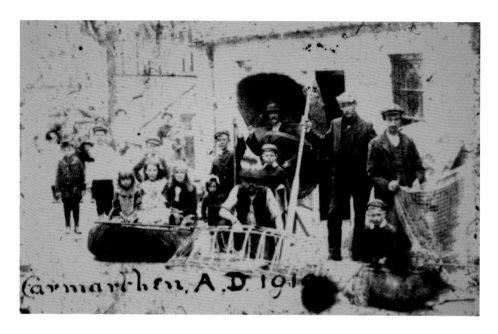

Coracles

Hide-covered boats were recorded by the Romans when they invaded Wales in AD 74, but no one is sure whether they were referring to the Irish *curragh* or the Welsh/British coracle. This delicate little craft has been used for fishing on the River Towy for centuries. Hundreds of coracles would be seen at the turn of the eighteenth and nineteenth centuries, fishing on the water and flitting in and out between the huge cargo ships at the Port of Carmarthen. At this time, it is estimated that some 2,000 townsfolk obtained their living from the river. From the top photograph, probably taken at Dan y Banc, it would appear that most of these coracle fishing families were very poor and living on the bread line. The lower picture is of a humorous postcard taking off the ancient British coracle fishermen.

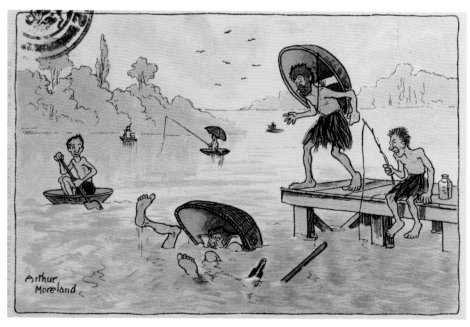

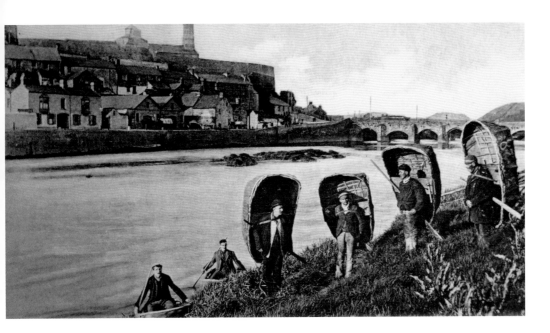

Coracles

Coracles, from the Welsh *cwrwgl*, have a history dating back thousands of years. Traditionally this delicate-looking little rivercraft is made from a framework of presoaked ash lathes held together with a basket-weave of willow. A seat is placed in the middle and the whole was originally covered in animal skins. The shape of the coracle on the River Towy has remained virtually unchanged over time and during the 1860s there were around 400 of these craft operating on the river. The top picture, with the view of Carmarthen Castle and Old Bridge in the background, was taken in 1898 during the fishing season which lasted from 1 March to 31 July each year. In contrast, the lower photograph of 29 August 2015 captures the coracle men preparing to enter the river from the wharf for the Carmarthen River Festival Coracle Races.

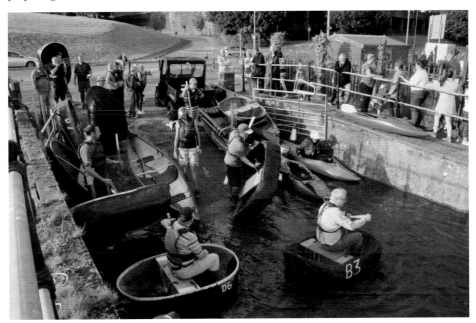

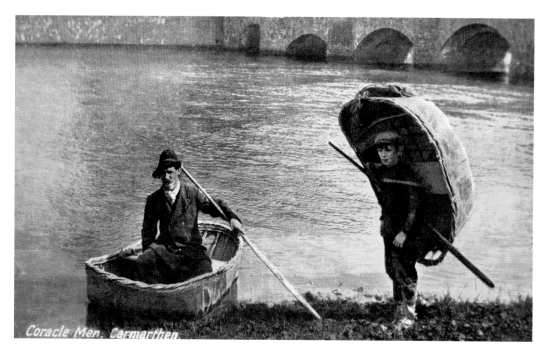

Coracle Men, Carmarthen.

Coracles

Two more progressive pictures, the top showing two coracle men in the 1860s preparing to fish on the river for salmon and sewin (sea trout), while the lower photograph shows competing coracle men preparing to do battle on the same river during the River Festival Coracle Races of August 2015.

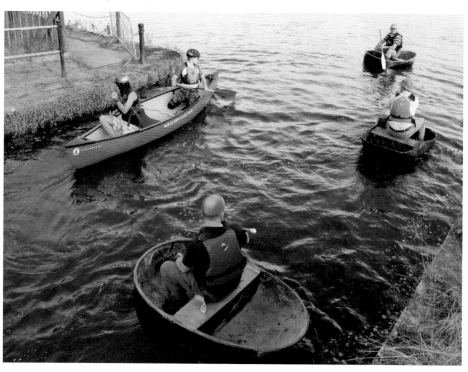

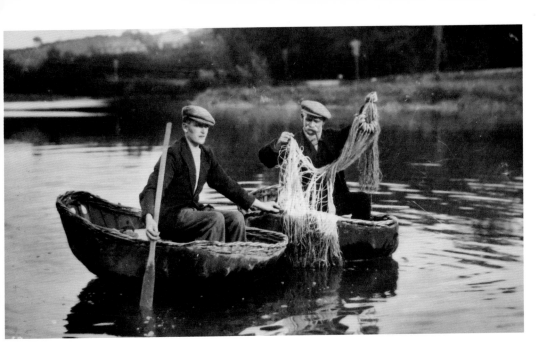

Coracles

As demonstrated in the top photograph, which probably dates from the early 1900s, fishing on the river was a two-man, two-coracle job. Usually carried out in the evening or night when the fish could not see their shadow or the net, a pair of coracles would gently float down the river with a net suspended between them held in one hand by each coracle man who skilfully controlled his vessel with an oar in the other hand. When a fish is caught, the two coracles are drawn together by pulling on the net. Not quite so gentile, the bottom photograph shows these intrepid young men in their boating machines paddling furiously to win in one of the fiercely contested coracle races held on the River Towy in August 2015.

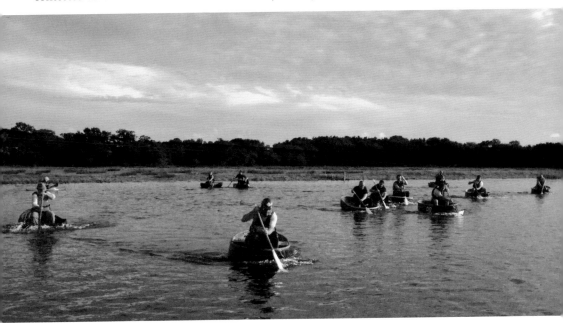

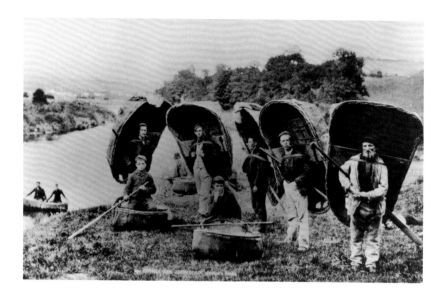

Coracles

Coracle building and sailing has been, and usually still is, a family concern with the skills handed down from generation to generation. In the top group photograph from the Carmarthen Coracle Museum Collection, the little boy sitting in the coracle in the middle is William Elias, the great-grandfather of Malcolm Rees, King of the River 2014. In the lower family photograph, also from the same collection, we have, from left to right, Raymond Rees MBE, (father of Malcolm Rees, King of the River 2014), William Elias BEM, (Malcolm's great-grandfather), and Owen Elias (son of William Elias). Both William Elias and Raymond Rees received recognition from the monarchs of their day for their services to Coracle Heritage and Fishing.

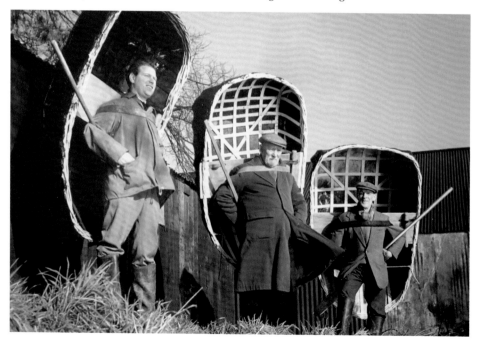

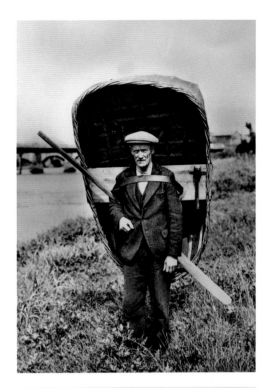

Coracles

The top picture is of William Elias BEM, taken around 1950. William received his accolade for services to coracles and their use for fishing in 1967. William Elias was Wales' oldest coracle man when he died in 1973 at the age of ninety-seven and was still fishing the Towy well into his eighties. The second photograph is of Malcolm Rees, great grandson of William Elias who has maintained the tradition of coracle fishing on the River Towy and the Carmarthenshire area. This picture was taken during the Carmarthen River Festival in August 2015. Malcolm holds one of the eight coracle fishing licences issued by the Natural Resources Wales organisation to protect fishing on the River Towy. Only two other rivers in West Wales support coracle fishing – the Rivers Teifi and Taf.

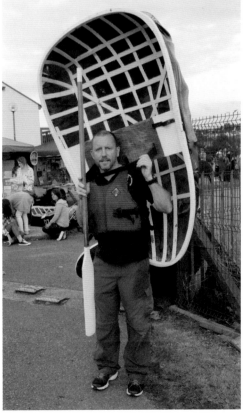

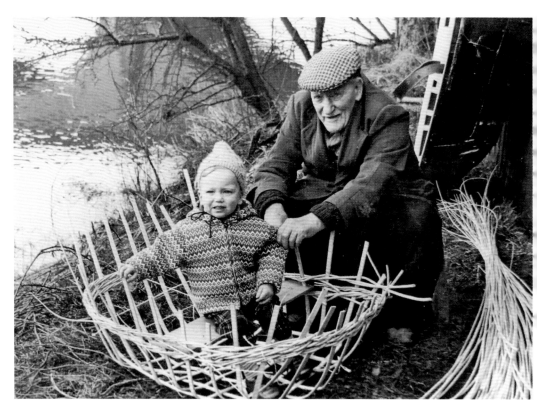

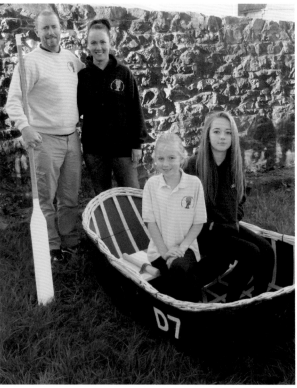

Coracles

Probably taken in 1968, the top photograph is of William Elias BEM with his great-grandson Malcolm Rees in a partially completed coracle, while the lower photograph replicates this with a picture taken of Malcolm with his wife Julie and children Jaymee and Mia, on 12 October 2015. Malcolm, an active coracle netsman, along with his wife Julie and other members of the Carmarthen Coracle and Netsmen's Association (established in 1938), ensure that the traditions of the coracle and coracle fishing are both protected and kept very much alive in the community. They have created a small museum and work with local schools and organisations, the wider community and help to organise the annual Carmarthen River Festival; they have even entertained royalty – namely Prince Charles in 2014.

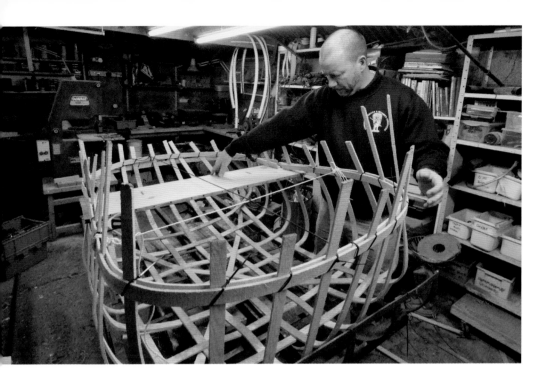

Coracles

In these two photographs taken in October 2015 in the small Carmarthen Coracle Museum, Malcolm Rees demonstrates both the construction of the coracle and the make-up and history of the different nets that have been used for coracle fishing over the ages.

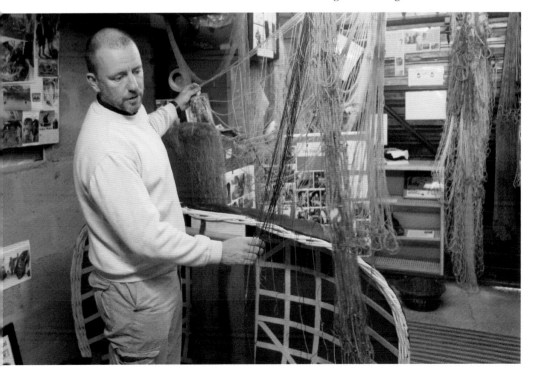

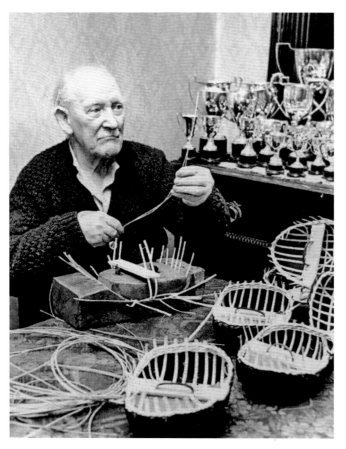

Coracles

Raymond Rees MBE was a well-known and respected coracle netsman and received his award for services to maintaining the traditions of the coracle and the craft of coracle-fishing. He was an active coracle fisherman until late in his life and sold coracle caught fish in his fishmonger shop in Carmarthen. Raymond was considered a fount of knowledge for all aspects of interest on the coracle and coracle fishing as well as an expert in making miniature coracles, an art which is now carried on by his daughter-in-law, Julie Rees. There is even a miniature coracle from the Carmarthen Coracle Museum in the White House, Washington DC.

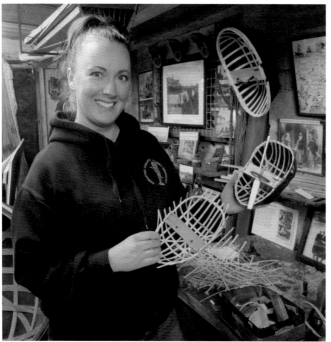

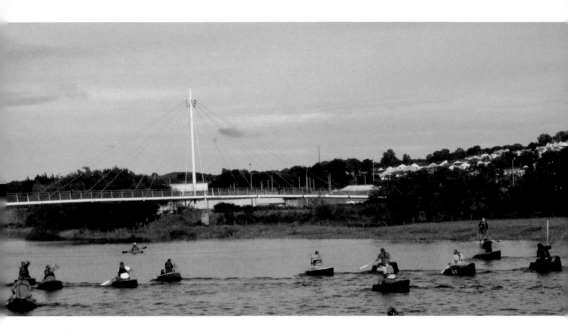

Pont King Morgan

The end of a perfect day with the coracle men paddling their way into history in one of the last races of the 2015 Carmarthen River Festival while the sun leaves its setting colours on the Pont King Morgan S-shaped lightweight pedestrian bridge and casts its reflection on the ebbing waters of the River Towy. This striking and eye-catching new cable-stay bridge was erected in 2005 at a cost of £2.8m to connect the centre of town to the railway station. The inset photograph shows a coracle mounted on the bridge in memory of eleven-year-old Cameron Comey who was lost to the river in February 2015. This tragedy led to the formation of the Carmarthenshire Water Safety Partnership, launched on 19 August 2015 by Christopher Salmon, police and crime commissioner in Dyfed-Powys.

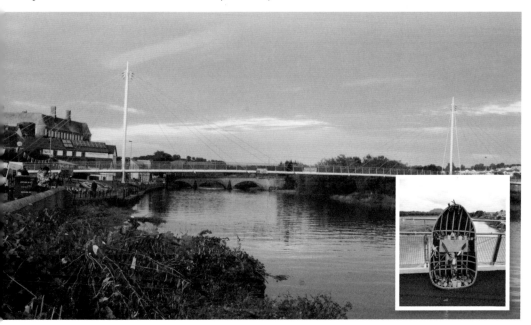

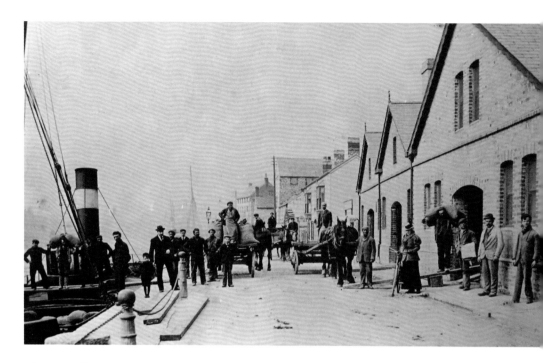

The Quayside

'Then and now'. The two photographs illustrate the changes that have taken place over time of the quayside in Carmarthen. The top picture, probably of the early 1900s, shows a very busy dock with a steam tug tied up at the jetty and a predominance of horse-drawn vehicles. Note the lady with the bicycle dressed in 'Emmeline Pankhurst' suffragette-style costume typical of the period. The lower photograph, taken by the author in October 2015, captures a much different scene where the quayside is now a roadway filled with motor vehicles.

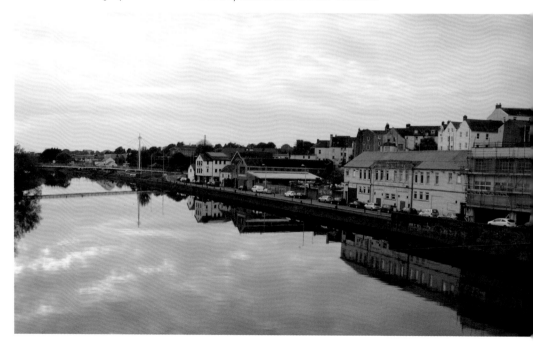

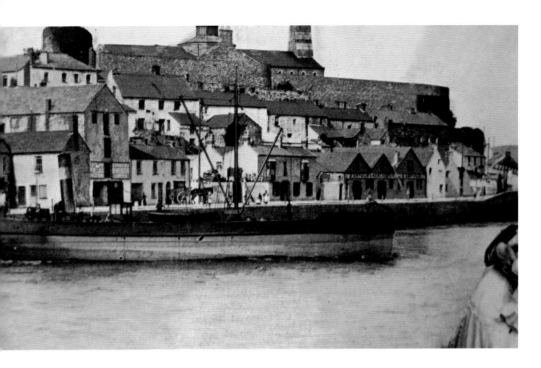

The Quayside

Another 'then and now' –two views of the Carmarthen quayside. Taken from a slightly different view point to that on the previous page, the first picture, of around 1900, is of the SS *Merthyr* berthed at the quayside with the castle towering above the dock in the background. The lower photograph, taken October 2015, shows the Towy Works erection that was completed in May 1909 on Bridge Street when it was still a thriving quay.

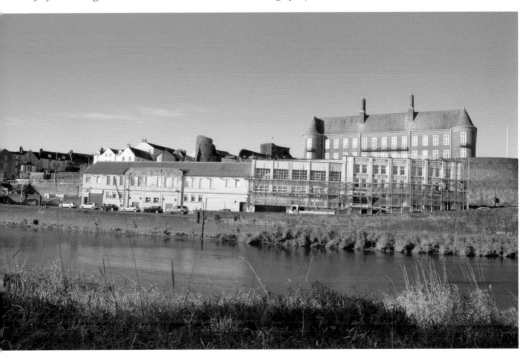

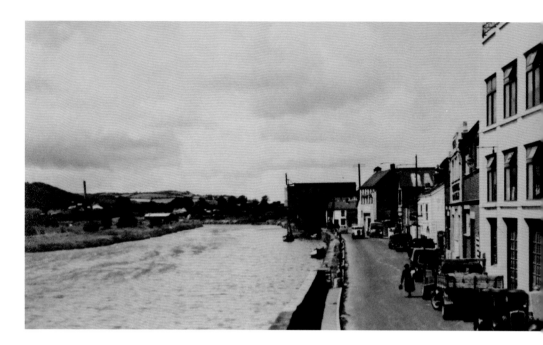

The Quayside

'An Eighth Wonder of the World', this was how the three-storeys-high Towy Works building (just visible on the right-hand side of the top photograph) was described in the *Carmarthen Journal* in 1909 when it was opened. Its architect, George Morgan of King Street, designer of the English Baptist chapel, Pentreporth School and the School of Art, had made maximum use of the elongated-shaped site, formerly a coal depot, to create this 'eighth wonder' which is shown having a 'makeover' in the lower photograph, taken in October 2015. Not to be confused, the legend 'Established 1795' carved over the warehouse door, relates to the original ironmongers shop in town that was incorporated into the Towy Works.

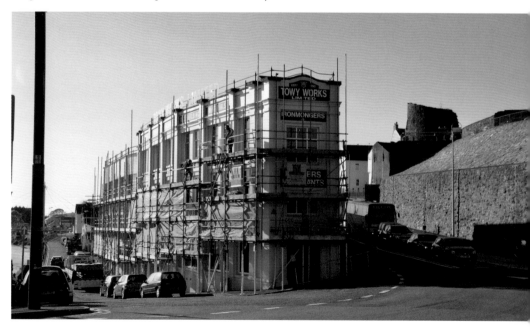

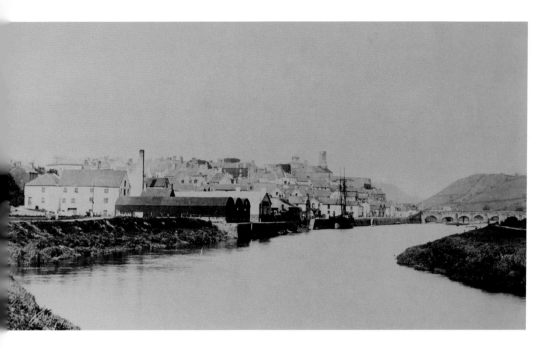

Carmarthen

Here are two interesting views of Carmarthen. The top photograph was taken in the early 1900s looking north along the River Towy towards the old road bridge with Merlin's Hill as a backcloth on one side and the castle and gaol on the other. There is a sailing ship berthed at the quayside and the Towy Works has yet to be built. The bottom picture is an aerial postcard view of 'Carmarthen and River Towy, from an aeroplane'. This would have been quite novel in its day as the photograph would have been taken between 1909, when the Towy Works was built, and 1936, when the Old River Bridge was demolished.

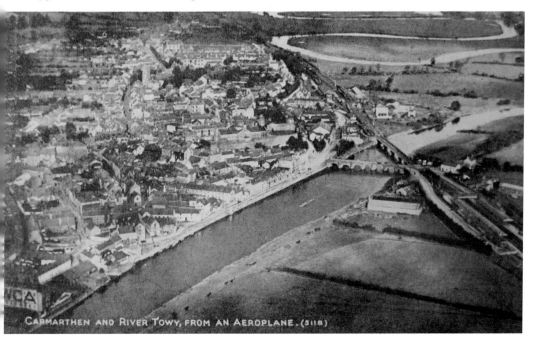

CARMARTHEN AND RIVER TOWY, FROM AN AEROPLANE. (5118)

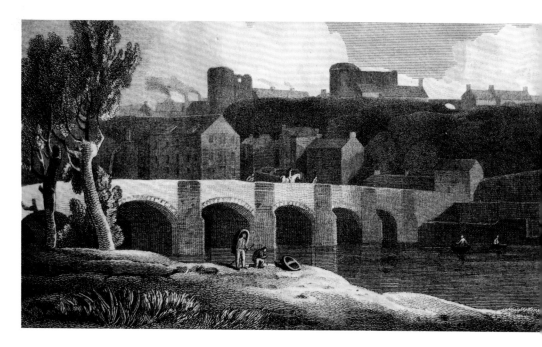

Carmarthen Bridge

The antique engraving of Carmarthen medieval bridge in the top picture was drawn by John Britton (1771–1857), antiquarian and topographer in around 1800. Britton specialised in preparing views of subjects from the opposite direction to what was considered by many other artists to be the subject's best side. This policy has been followed in this sketch of the Old Bridge, which has been viewed looking down stream with the castle and gaol in the background. The bottom photograph of the old Carmarthen Bridge was taken between 1909 and 1936 from the 'conventional' direction looking upstream.

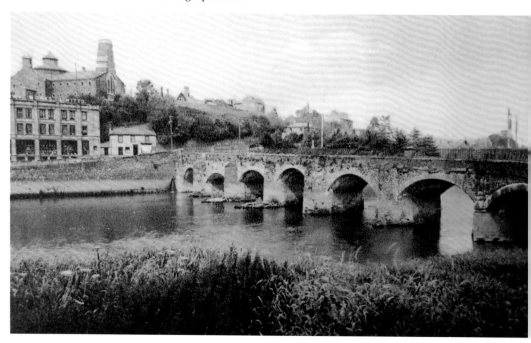

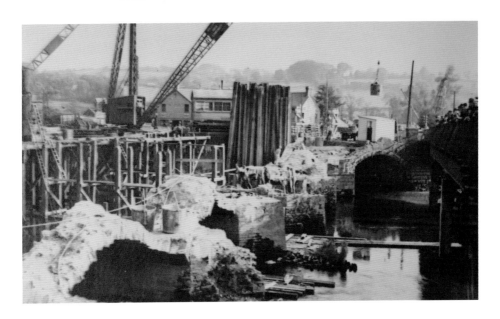

Carmarthen Bridge

There was probably a wooden bridge over the River Towy at this point in Roman times. If so, it had certainly gone by 1188 when Giraldus Cambrenis visited the town. The first stone bridge is not recorded until 1233 and was probably built during the siege of Carmarthen in that year. The old bridge had seven arches and an iron balustrade. It had been repaired and widened many times, but eventually the bridge was declared unsuitable for traffic and demolished in 1936. The present three-arch concrete-structured road bridge was designed in 1933 by architect Clough Williams-Ellis (the designer of Portmeirion). Construction started in May 1936 and the bridge was completed by September 1937 at a cost of £89.91. It was officially opened in April 1938 by the Minister of Transport, Leslie Burgin. The top photograph shows demolition of the old bridge underway. This view was taken in 1936 from the temporary bridge erected alongside the old bridge, while the lower picture of July 2015 shows the road bridge as we know it today.

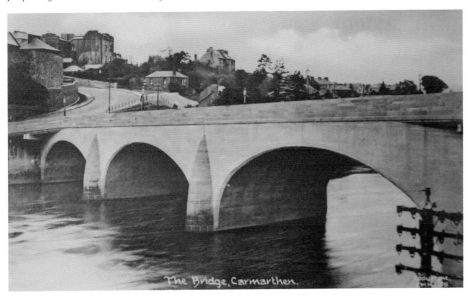

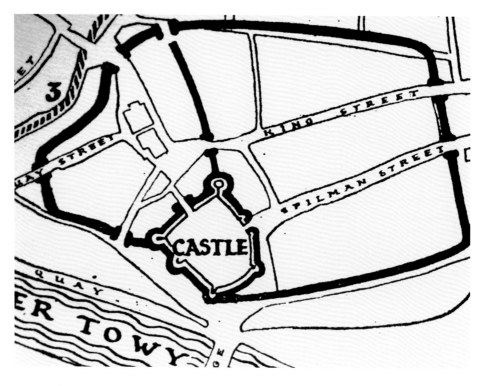

Carmarthen Castle, County Gaol and County Hall

The plan for Carmarthen Castle, county gaol and/county hall can be seen in the top view (attributed and credited to Malcolm and Edith Lodwick), which shows the town walls and castle of Carmarthen in Norman and medieval times. The town walls were probably built to follow the boundaries of the castle bailey and, as such, would have formed part of the castle's defence system. In 1093/4, it is recorded that the Norman William Fitz Baldwin built a fortification in the vicinity of the present castle site, the latter having been in use since 1105. Following the examples of the Romans (the site of the Roman fort falls within the boundary of the castle bailey), the castle was sited strategically overlooking the upper tidal limit of the River Towy and would have originally been of the classic Norman motte-and-bailey design. The present Carmarthenshire County Council Hall was erected in 1955 on Castle Hill, largely destroying parts of Carmarthen Castle and all of the county gaol.

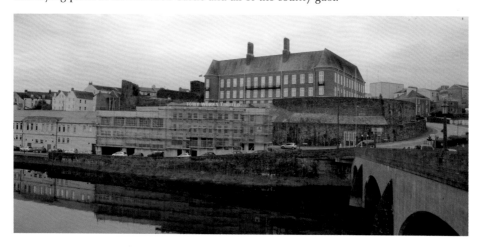

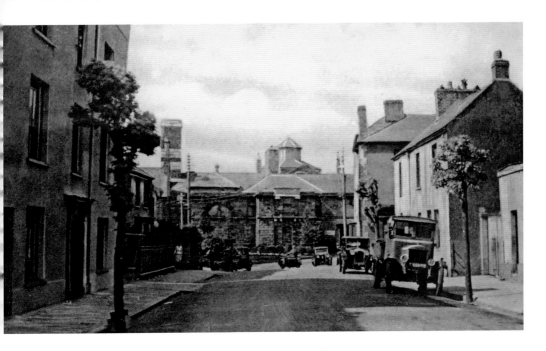

Carmarthenshire County Council Hall and County Gaol

Travelling towards town along Spilman Street pre-1938, one would have seen what was once the Carmarthenshire County Gaol at the far end. The gaol was closed in 1922 and in 1938 it was demolished to make way for the new Carmarthenshire County Council Hall. It is this building (captured in the lower photograph of July 2015) that the traveller now sees when walking along the same route today. The county hall was designed by Percy Thomas in 1935 with site clearance probably starting in 1938 when the gaol was demolished, but the building was not completed until 1955.

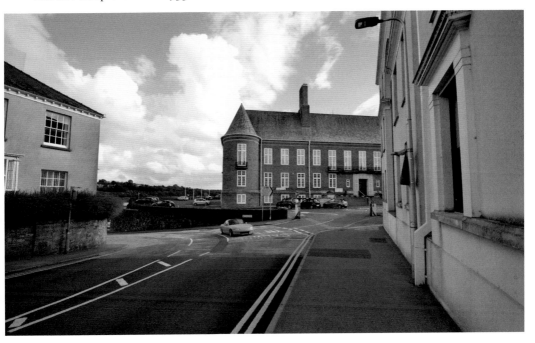

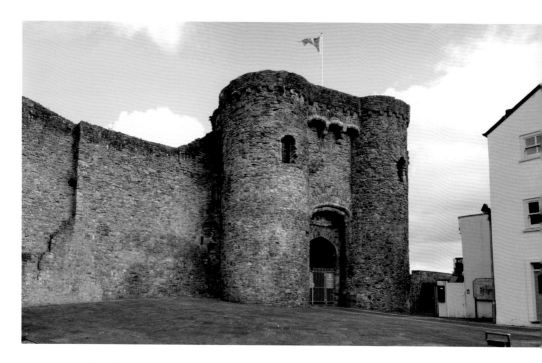

Carmarthen Castle

Two photographs on this page, both taken in July 2015, show the major remains of Carmarthen Castle that were left standing after the development and construction on Castle Hill of the Carmarthenshire County Council Hall during the period 1938–1948. What is left of the castle structure and these remains today is as a result of the repairs it received in 1774 (the royal auditor had reported it 'quite demolished' in 1660) and any alterations that were during to them the building of the County Gaol in 1789–92.

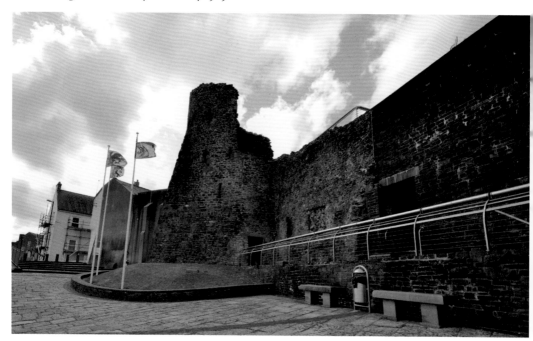

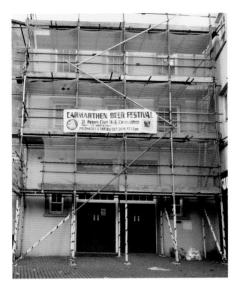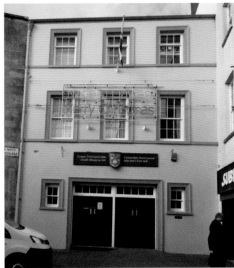

St Peter's Civic Hall

St Peter's Civic Hall, No. 1, Nott Square, was acquired by St Peter's parish, converted into a hall and opened as a church house in 1916, at a cost of over £2,500. In 1964, the rear wall and foundations of the building were found to be unsafe and it was demolished and rebuilt in contemporary style. The Church in Wales sold the church house to the Carmarthen Town Council in the 1970s. Today, St Peter's Civic Hall, as well as housing the Carmarthen Town Council Offices and mayor's chamber, continues to be run as a town centre amenity, a premier venue for concerts, eisteddfodau, plays, conferences, coffee mornings, etc. The top two photographs are of Peter's Civic Hall before and after it went through its latest facelift in 2015. In the lower photograph, the Mayor, Cllr Barry Williams, and town clerk, Alun J. Harries, are seen discussing council business in the council office, 22 September 2015.

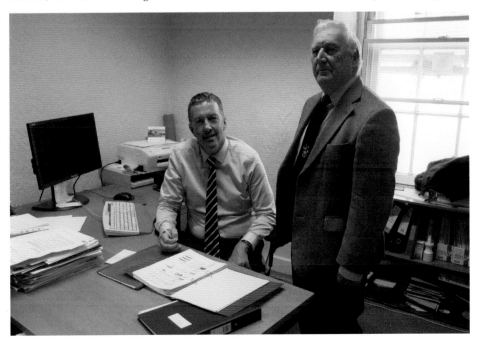

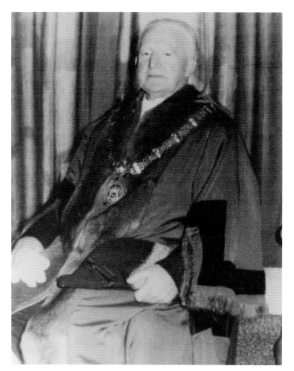

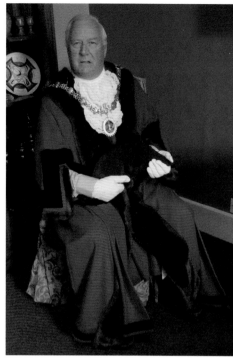

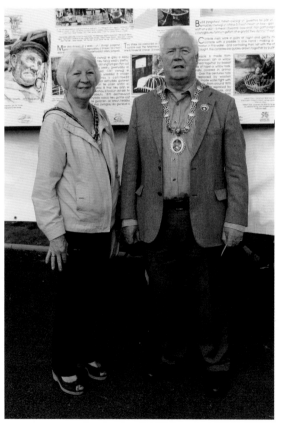

The Mayor of Carmarthen

In around the 1300s, Carmarthen was the largest Welsh town with a population of around 1,000. Just over 200 years later in 1546, it was made a corporate borough with an appointed mayor and common council. Following a chequered history through time, in 1974 after the Local Government Act was abolished, Carmarthen Borough Council was reformed as Carmarthen Town Council. The first mayor of this new town council for 1974–75 was Cllr Ivor Morgan Morris, while the current mayor for 2015–16 is Cllr Barry Williams. These two mayors are respectively pictured alongside each other in the top photographs. In the lower photograph, the current mayor of Carmarthen town, Cllr Barry Williams is shown with his consort, Mrs Barbara Williams, at the 2015 Carmarthen River Festival.

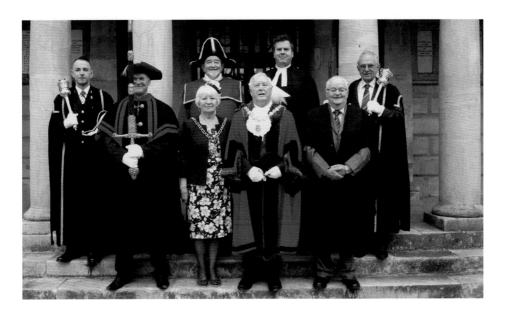

Mayor-Making Ceremony

On Friday, 15 May 2015, at the Mayor-Making Ceremony in the Guildhall, Cllr Barry Williams became the mayor of Carmarthen town for 2015–16. The two pictures show firstly, the new mayor posing on the steps of the guildhall with his consort, Mrs Barbara Williams, other civic dignitaries and the town sword-bearer, and secondly, with the town sword-bearer in front, striding up Hall Street towards Nott Square. Carmarthen is the only town in Wales which, by Royal Grant of 1546, has the privilege of having a sword carried before its mayor on occasions of state. Together with the town's two maces, the sword presented to the town in 1564 as a gift from one Richard Birtt, is only allowed to be paraded for the Mayor-Making Ceremony, Mayor Sunday, Remembrance Sunday and the town council Christmas service. For peacetime parades the sword is sheathed; however, in wartime it is paraded bare.

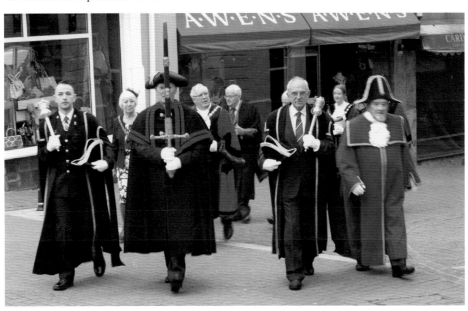

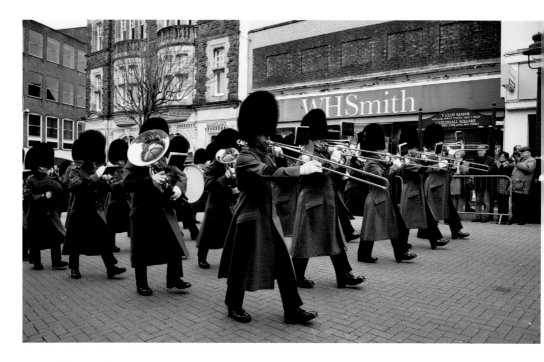

The Welsh Guards

Welsh Guard have a long association with Carmarthen. In 2010, they exercised their Freedom of the Town and as shown in the top picture (Carmarthen *Journal*), they are captured marching through Guild Hall Square on 16 January 2013 following their return from a tour of duty in Afghanistan. To celebrate the 100th anniversary of the founding of the Welsh Guards in 1915, they marched through Carmarthen again on 29 September 2015, and paraded in Guild Hall Square for inspection, as shown in the lower photograph.

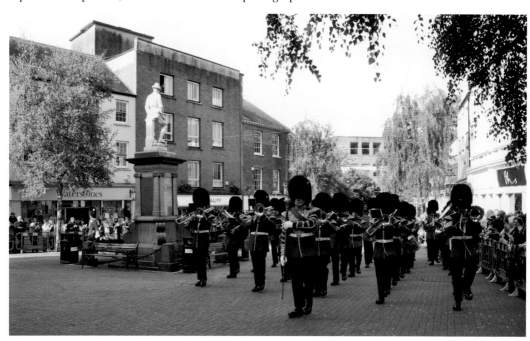

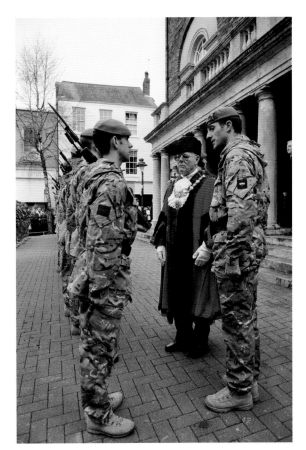

The Welsh Guards

In the top photograph, taken in January 2013 (*Carmarthen Journal*), the Mayor, Cllr Philip Grice (2012–13) is seen talking to the guardsmen and chatting, no doubt, about their experiences during the recent tour of duty in Afghanistan. The lower photograph, taken by the author on 29 September 2015, is of the Welsh Guards preparing for an Inspection Parade in front of the Guild Hall during the celebrations of the 100th anniversary of the founding of the Welsh Guards in 1915.

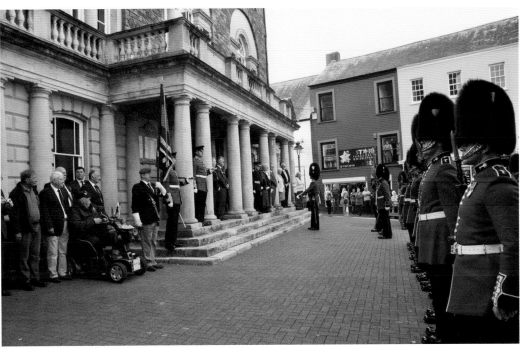

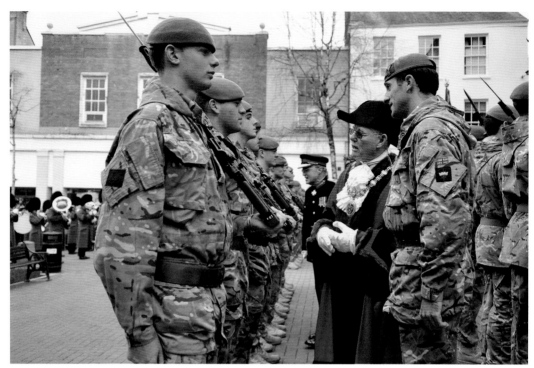

Welsh Guards

Two more photographs of the Welsh Guards on inspection parade on Guild Hall Square. The top photograph (*Carmarthen Journal*) is another shot of the Mayor, Cllr Philip Grice (2012–13), chatting to the soldiers who were dressed for this coming-home parade in their khaki field dress. In contrast, the Welsh Guards are resplendent in their Bearskins and Best Red Uniforms for the 100th anniversary parade through Carmarthen on 29 September 2015. Also resplendent in his red robes is the Mayor of Carmarthen, Cllr Barry Williams (2015–16) as he proceeds to inspect the parade on 29 September 2015.

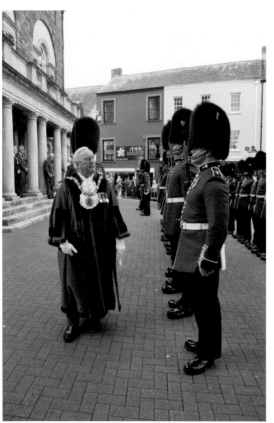

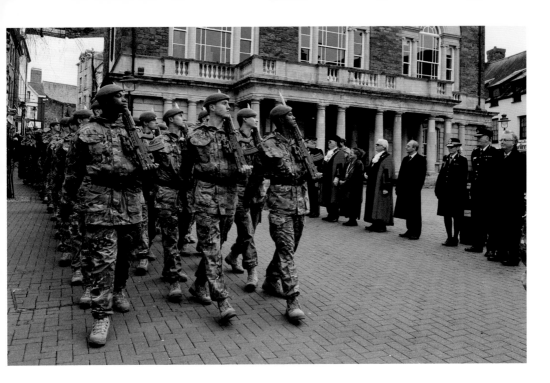

Welsh Guards

The return leg of the march through town to the barracks at Picton Terrace, the Welsh Guards march past the line-up of dignitaries in Guild Hall Square and receive an accolade from them and the crowd. The two photographs were respectively taken in January 2013 (*Carmarthen Journal*) and September 2015

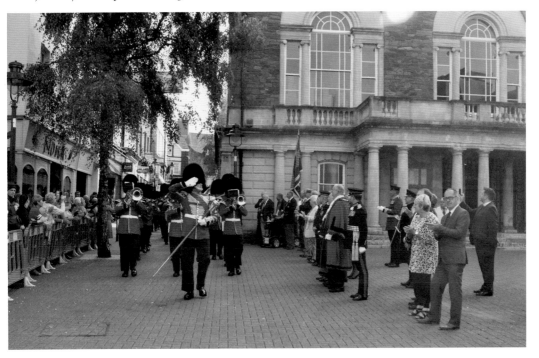

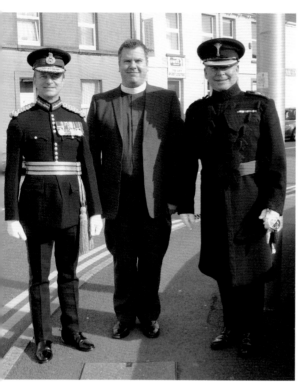

Welsh Guards

The top photograph was taken by the author following the 100th Anniversary Parade of the Welsh Guards through Carmarthen on 29 September 2015, and shows, left to right, Major General Talbot Rice, Regimental Lieutenant Colonel of the Welsh Guards, Revd Canon Leigh Richardson, Priest-in-Charge, Parish of St Peter's, and Colonel Tom Brown, Regimental Adjutant, RHQ Welsh Guards. Major General Talbot Rice who is the Patron of The Friends of St Peter's, is also a direct descendant of Sir Rhys ap Thomas, one of Britain's Tudor heroes whose tomb is in St Peter's church (see page 82). The lower two photographs, taken at the Concert given in St' Peter's church by the Welsh Guards Band on 28 September 2015, are of the Mayor of Carmarthen, Cllr Barry Williams, with Bandmaster Warrant Officer 1 Richard Burton, and Senior Director of Music Lieutenant Colonel Kevin F. N. Roberts.

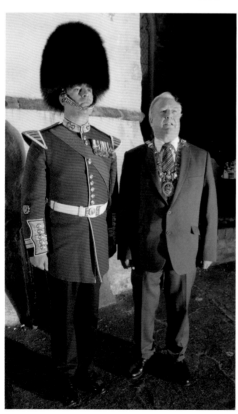

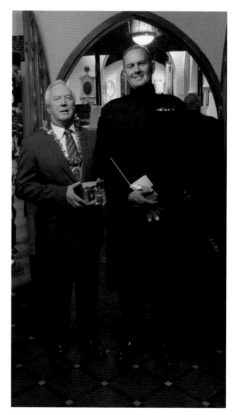

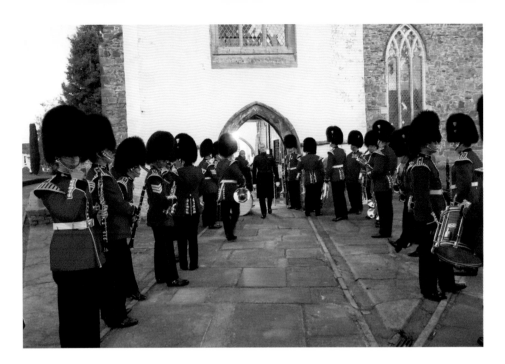

The Welsh Guards Concert

As part of the their 100th anniversary of the regiment's foundation, the Band of the Welsh Guards gave a concert on the night of 28 September 2015 in St Peter's church. In the top photograph, band members are waiting with their Director of Music, Lieutenant Colonel Kevin F. N. Roberts, to parade into the church, in the lower picture, the band are seen marching in to delight and entertain a full and appreciative audience.

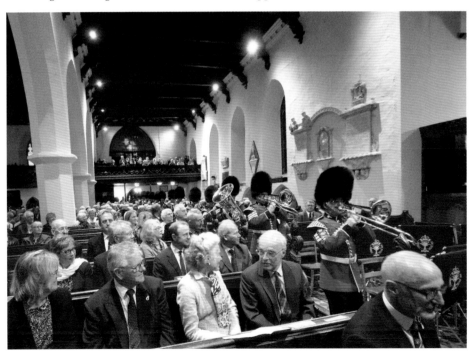

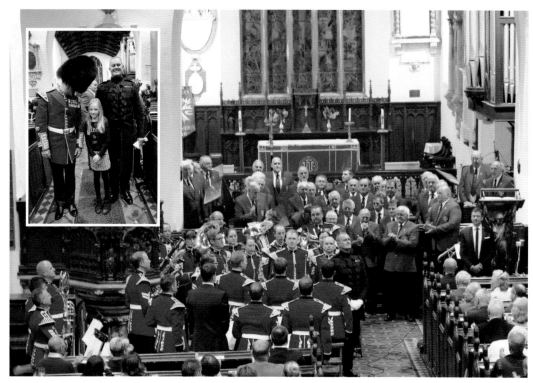

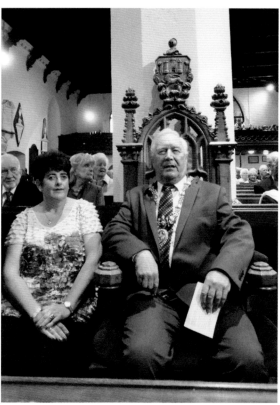

The Welsh Guards Concert

The Welsh Guards Concert Band and their Director of Music, Lieutenant Colonel Kevin F. N. Roberts, receiving an accolade from the audience, the Haverfordwest Male Voice Choir, Musical Director Richard Stephens, and Soloist Mark Llewellyn Evans, after giving a splendid concert at St Peter's church on 28 September 2015 to celebrate the 100th anniversary of the regiment's foundation. During this performance, and as recorded in the lower left-hand photograph, the Mayor of Carmarthen, Cllr Barry Williams, took advantage of his right and privilege to occupy the 1851 Mayor's chair. Not quite so privileged to have a seat all to herself, but equally pleased, was would be Welsh Guards Bands-woman Mia Rees, who had the honour to be photographed with the Band's Director of Music, Lieutenant Colonel Kevin F. N. Roberts and Bandmaster Warrant Officer 1 Richard Burton.

St Peter's Church

St Peter's church, the original parish church of Carmarthen, is one of the largest churches in the diocese of St David's. The date of its foundation is unknown, but as it is dedicated to St Peter and not a Celtic saint, this may indicate a Norman foundation, possibly shortly after the construction of the castle in around 1109. As such, it is the oldest building in the town that is still in use for its original purpose. It lies just within the boundary of the Roman town of Moridunum which continued to exist into the late fourth century. The left-hand picture and inset compare the church's three-storeyed tower with the first photograph having been taken some time after 1879 when the Lych Gate was erected in memory of the Revd Latimer Maurice Jones, vicar (1863–77). The second photograph which highlights the white limewash probably applied during the 1903–05 renovation of the tower, was taken in October 2015. Note how the trees have grown during the intervening period of time between when these photographs were taken. The lower photograph taken looking east along the nave towards the chancel, probably dates to the 1930s and before electric lighting was installed.

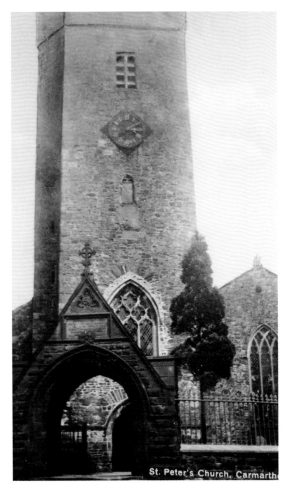

St. Peter's Church, Carmarth[en]

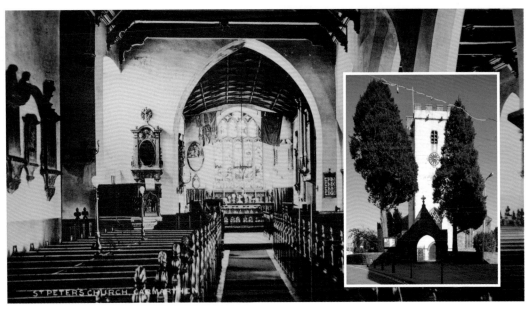

ST PETER'S CHURCH, CARMARTHEN

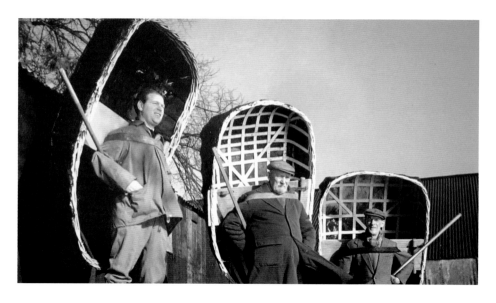

St Peter's Church

This interesting photograph was possibly taken in 1976 either before or after the bells had been renovated and before they were rehung in a new steel frame. According to the church history, the bells were previously rehung in 1904, at which time two more bells were added to complete a ring of eight. The bottom photograph and accompanying sketch is of the tomb of Sir Rhys ap Thomas, K. G., who died in 1525 in Carmarthen Friary. He was originally buried in the friary, but following the Dissolution of the Monasteries in 1538, his tomb and contents were moved to St Peter's church. His descendant, Lord Dynevor, heavily restored the tomb in 1866 and it was placed in its present position in 1886. The two Tudor effigies of Sir Rhys and his lady are original and represent the ancient style of full-length figures overlaying the bodies and tomb. Sir Rhys is an important figure in the annals of British history having killed King Richard III at the Battle of Bosworth Field on 22nd August 1485, an act that ensured that Henry Tudor was crowned King of England (see publication *The Man Who Killed Richard* III by Susan Fern, Amberley Publishing).

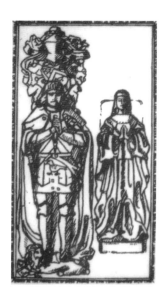

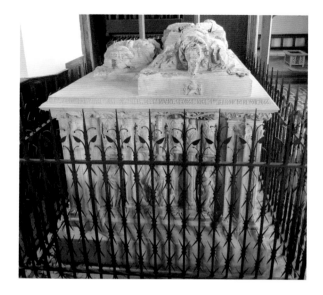

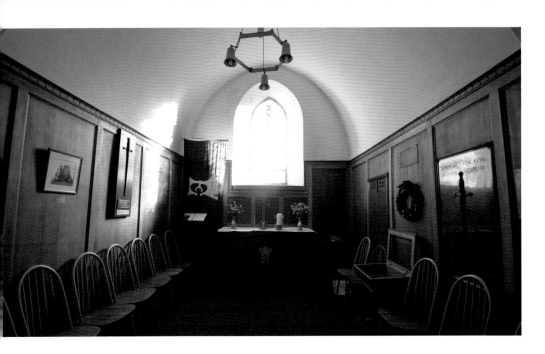

Peter's Church – Old Grammar School Chapel

This photograph was taken in October 2015 and shows the Old Grammar School Chapel that occupies what was once the Chapel of Rest on the south side of the south aisle of the church. It was dedicated in October 1969 to those boys and masters of the Old Grammar School that gave their lives in both world wars and other conflicts that have followed. The lower picture is of a postcard inscribed 'Intermediate Schools', Carmarthen, and was probably taken in the 1930s. As the blue plaque of the inset records, The Queen Elizabeth Grammar School for Boys, founded in 1576, was at this site from 1884 to 1978. It is no longer a school, but celebrated its 400th anniversary in 1976.

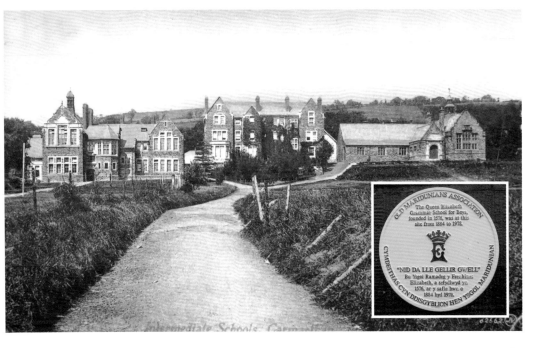

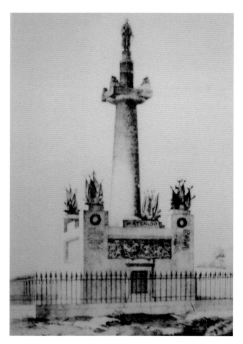

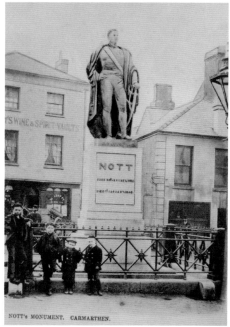

NOTT's MONUMENT. CARMARTHEN.

Picton and Nott Memorials

Carmarthen seems to abound with memorials, the two most important of which are those of Lieutenant General Sir Thomas Picton, GCB, and General Sir William Nott.

General Picton died instantly due to being hit in the head by a musket ball at the Battle of Waterloo on 18 June 1815. The first Picton Monument (top left photograph) was built by public subscription in 1827. It was designed by John Nash with decoration by E. H. Baily. The monument was demolished in 1846 and replaced by the present obelisk (not shown). The first monument, frieze, shown in the lower picture, was recovered from a garden in Johnstown and is on display in the Carmarthen Museum. On the left-hand side, it shows General Picton falling from his horse into the arms of a soldier of the Highland Division. The statue of General Nott is in Nott Square and was erected in 1851. Nott earned a name and reputation for himself as a British military leader in British India. It is reputed that his bronze statue was cast from cannon captured at the Battle of Maharajpur, India.

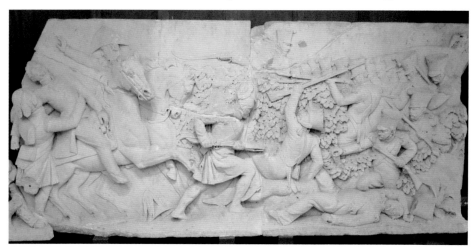

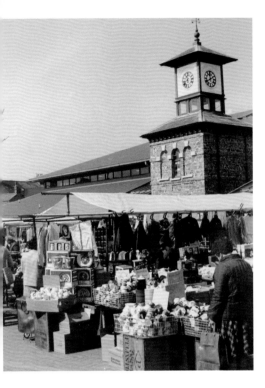
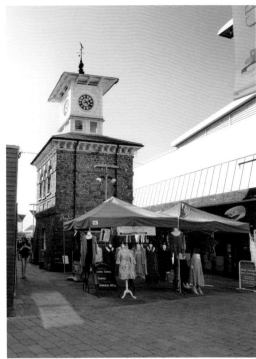

Carmarthen Markets

The iconic Market Clock Tower was built as part of the new Carmarthen Market in 1846 and is now a Grade II-Listed Building. Even though the old market building was demolished in 2009 to make way for a new market, the Clock Tower is still there today. Compare the two top photographs; the one on the left was taken in the 1950s or 1960s while the one on the right was taken in October 2015. The two lower pictures show respectively left to right, the hustle and bustle in the provisions market and livestock market, both probably taken in the post-war period.

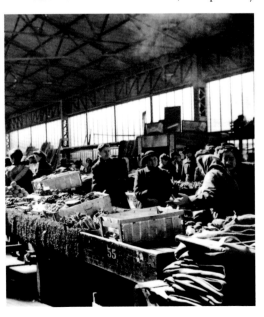
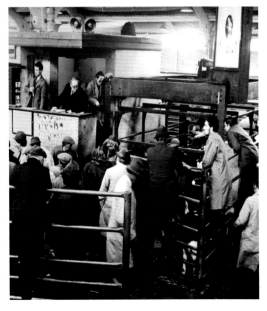

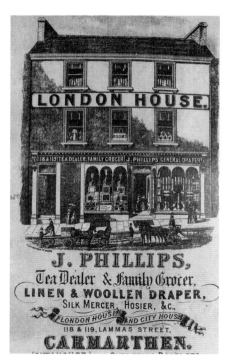

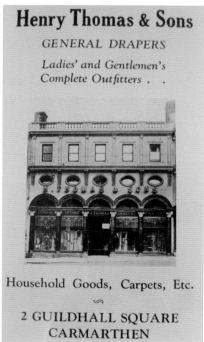

Trade Advertisments

Of the four businesses 'advertised' on this page, only one has survived the ravages of 'business time', and that is Evans & Watkins of Hill Street, founded in the 1920s, who are thankfully still trading today as a traditional gentleman's outfitters shop. The big hat sign shown in the bottom left-hand photograph taken of No. 14 Lammas Street in November 2015 survives to record the once important trade of beaver-skin hats carried on the premises there by Evan Morris & Sons, men's clothiers 1897.

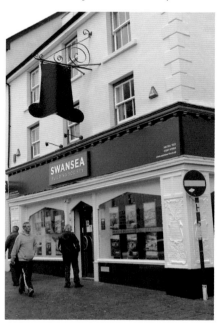

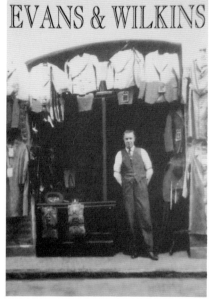

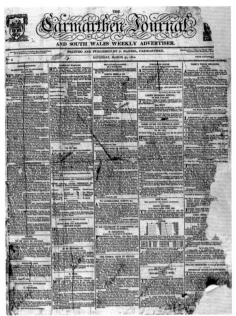

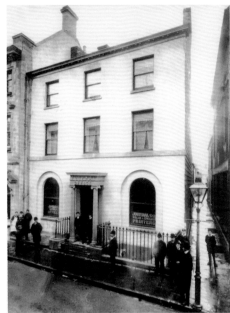

The *Carmarthen Journal*

The *Carmarthen Journal* was founded in 1810 and is the oldest newspaper in Wales. The top left picture is of the front page of the oldest surviving copy of the *Carmarthen Journal* for 31 March 1810, while alongside on the right is a photograph of the newspaper's first office in King Street. The 'Journal Office' is carved on the front portal. This building was demolished to make way for the building of the post office, at which time the *Carmarthen Journal* moved into the present premises (bottom picture) of which it now only uses a small part.

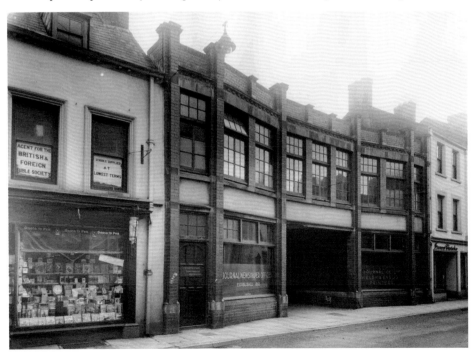

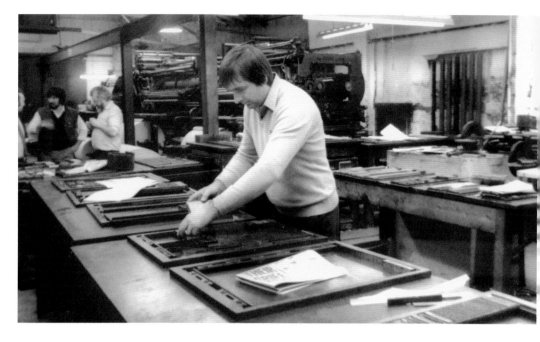

The *Carmarthen Journal*

A thing of the past, the top picture shows a printer preparing for typesetting in the *Journal*'s offices in around 1985. This process has now gone digital and with the removal of the printing presses, the *Carmarthen Journal* has been able to release accommodation in the building and downsize to just a street-front facility. The latter is shown in the lower photograph with news manager Lee MacGregor, standing in the doorway of the *Carmarthen Journal* reception office. The lower picture alongside is of the front page of the Wednesday 3 March 2010 issue of the *Carmarthen Journal* celebrating the 200th anniversary of the paper's founding in 1810.

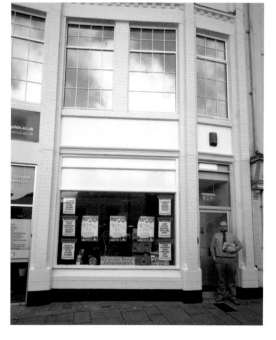

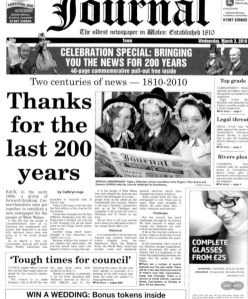

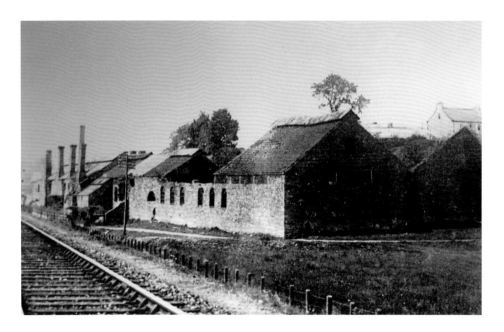

Carmarthen Iron and Tinplate Works

In 1748, Robert Morgan arrived in Carmarthen and built the Carmarthen Iron and Tinplate Works. On land leased from Lady Trevor, Morgan had started erecting his ironworks at the end of 1748 on a site just outside of what was the built-up area of the town at that time. This site was on a small stream towards Tanerdy to the north-east of the town and located on the banks of the River Towy on the south side and the main highway to Llandeilo and the West, on the north side. The raw materials of coal and iron ore were transported to the works by both road and small coastal vessels by river. The upper photograph is a very early picture taken of the works after the tinplate works had been introduced to the site (between 1750 and 1777) and the railway built (1858). The lower photograph, taken in 2014, shows some of the existing old works buildings which are still in use on the site today.

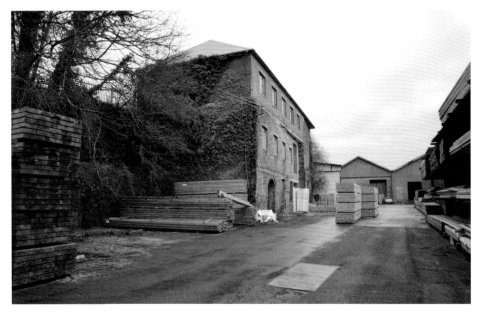

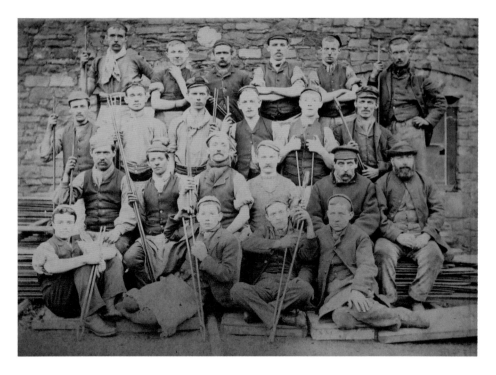

Carmarthen Iron and Tinplate Works

One motley bunch, captured by the camera for all time in the early top picture, are tinplate workers, characterised by their metal tongs, employed at the old Carmarthen Tinplate Works. Morgan developed the works with the erection of a blast furnace (in 1747), forge, rolling-mills and tin-mills (in 1761) with the end product of his works bearing the family's esteemed stamp and trademark M. C. (Morgan, Carmarthen) becoming famous throughout many parts of Europe. and Russia. For a period, the furnace produced canon for the Board of Ordnance. The lower photograph, taken in July 2014 2015, shows what remains are left of some of these old workings, which will require an archaeological survey and dig to determine their true purpose and locate such items as the blast furnace and waterwheel motive power.

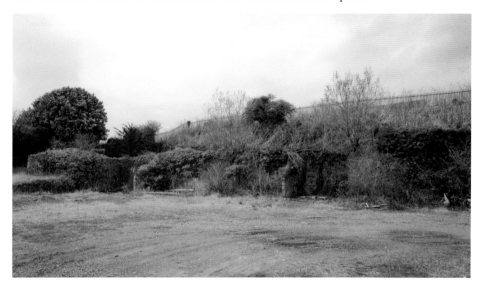

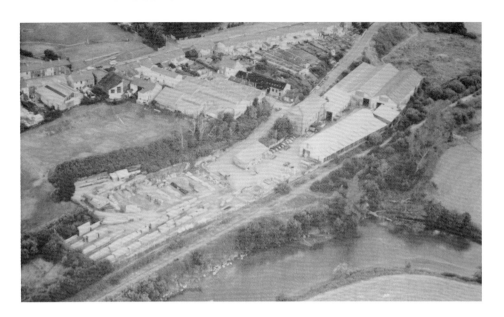

Carmarthen Iron and Tinplate Works

In 1771, Robert Morgan purchased the mills and furnace from Lady Trevor for £3,000. He died in 1778 and was succeeded by a number of members of the Morgan family. The tinworks are recorded as producing tinplate in 1805 and of exporting orders of 500 boxes of tinplate to Glasgow in 1823. Messrs Reynolds & Smith eventually took over the business and in 1826, when the works were working at full pressure to meet the increasing orders for tinplates, moved to Aberavon, causing great anxiety to the community at Carmarthen. Jewson, the general builder's merchant eventually took over and expanded the site, as shown in the top aerial photograph, which was taken before 1968 when the Roman Fort, top left of the photograph, was excavated. Many of the Old Tinplate Works buildings were taken over and are still in use today, as shown in the lower picture of 2014, albeit, they now have new roofs. The inset photograph is of Furnace House, King Street, the one-time residence of Carmarthen ironmasters Robert and John Morgan. The railings bear the inscribed date 1761.

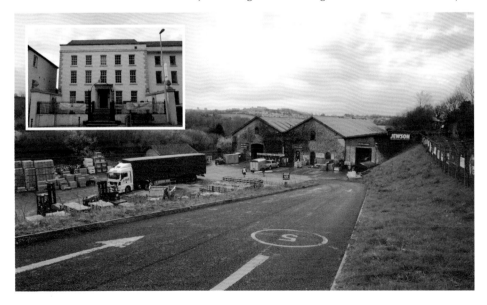

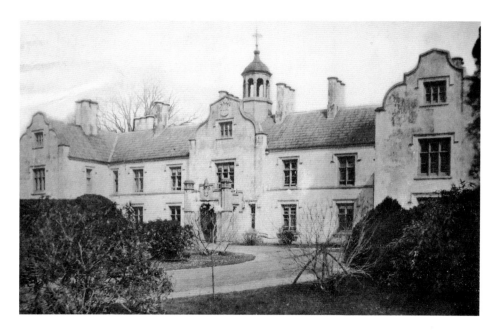

The Bishop's Palace, Abergwili

The village of Abergwili is known for its Bishop's Palace. The latter has been home to the Bishop of St David's since 1542 when Bishop William Barlow transferred his palace here from St David's. It was believed to have been built between 1283 and 1291 as a college of priests when Thomas Bek was made bishop of St David's. Following a disastrous fire in 1903, the palace was almost completely rebuilt and contains intact, the chapel added by Archbishop Laud in 1625. The top photograph, probably before the fire of 1903, shows the front of the palace with the bell tower still in-situ. The lower picture is of Bishop William Basil Jones with his family at the palace. He was bishop of Pembrey, St David's, from 1874 until he died at Abergwili in 1897.

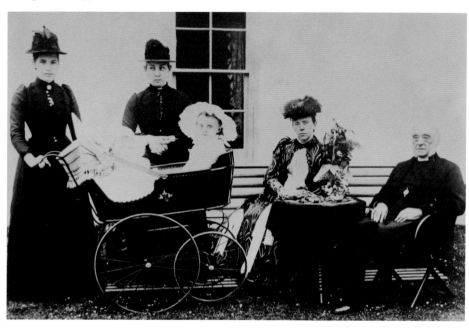

The Bishop's Palace and County Museum, Abergwili

In 1974, the old Episcopal palace was purchased by Carmarthenshire County Council for use as a museum, while a new residence for the bishops, 'Llys Esgob', together with diocesan offices, were built in part of the old palace grounds. The Carmarthenshire County Museum, shown in the top photograph at its original premises in Nos 4–5, Quay Street, Carmarthen, is now housed in the Old Bishop's Palace complete with all the original historic décor of this 'palatial' premises. The lower photograph of the Old Bishop's Palace, was taken on 30 June 2015.

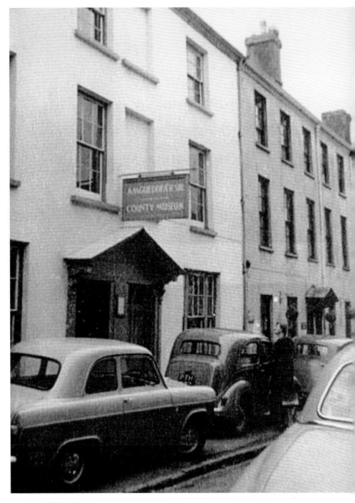

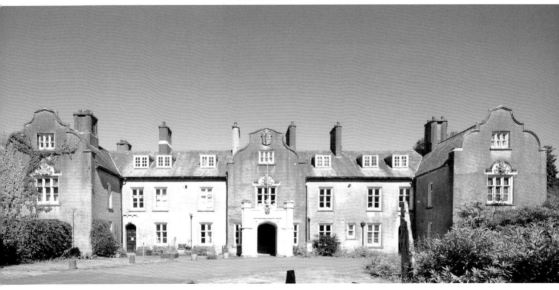

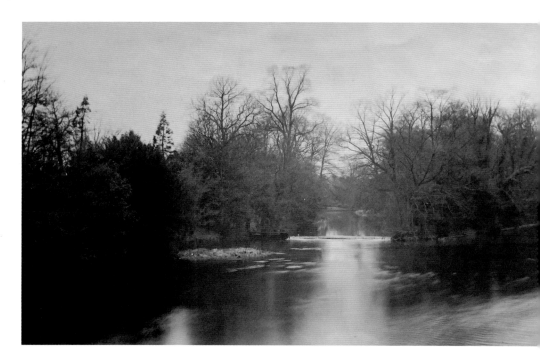

The Bishop's Pond

Until 1802, the River Towy flowed past the back of the Old Bishop's Palace. At this time, it changed its course and left an isolated 'oxbow' lake, which was named the Bishop's Pond. As can be seen by comparing the two photographs of around 1900 (top picture) and today (2 October 2015), the lake is overgrown and ever so slowly silting up so that one day it will eventually become a meadow again. In the meantime, it is a large lily pond and home to many varieties of flora and fauna.

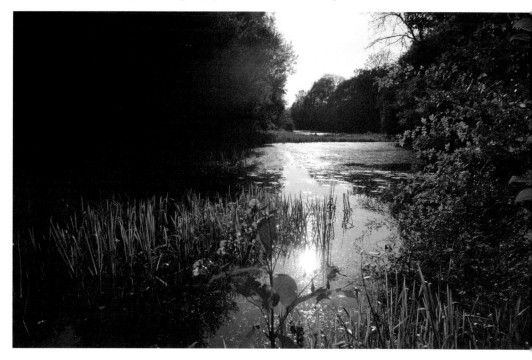

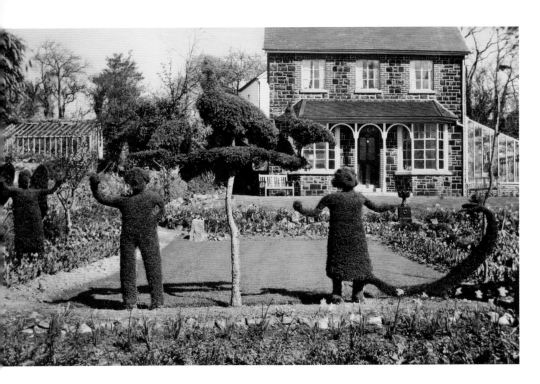

The Garden of Eden

The Garden of Eden at Abergwili was once a very busy and major tourist attraction in the area, displaying biblical figures and animals all created by topiary – the art of clipping shrubs, bushes and hedges into ornamental shapes. It is no longer a visitor attraction, but still, no doubt, paradise to the present owners of the property.

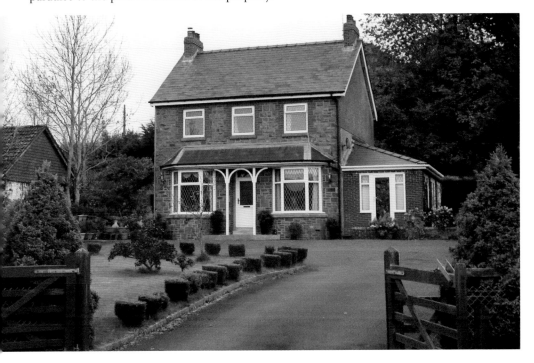

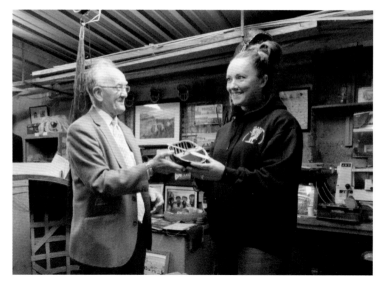

Miniature Coracles
The author being presented with a miniature coracle by model-maker extraordinaire, Julie Rees of the Carmarthen Coracle & Netsmen's Association. Julie is carrying on the art and tradition established by her famous father-in-law and coracle man, Raymond Rees, MBE.

Acknowledgements

In compiling and preparing this book, I am grateful for the all the assistance and support that I have received from the following organisations and individuals, for which I offer my sincerest thanks and gratitude.

First and foremost, Gavin Evans Esq., Curator and Staff of Carmarthenshire County Museum, Abergwili, who have given me free access to their photographic archive at the Old Bishop's Palace; Julie and Malcolm Rees of the Carmarthen Coracle & Netsmen's Association who have filled my coffers with an abundance of images from their wonderful collection of coracle and associated photographs; Ken Murphy Esq., Director of the Dyfed Archaeological Trust; Phillip Wait Esq., Designer, Cambria Archaeology; Sharon and Gareth Richards, Merlin's Hill Centre, Alltyfyrddin Farm, Abergwili; Carys Richards, The Merlin's Hill Wool Collection; Emma Bryant, editor, and Lee MacGregor Esq., news editor, *Carmarthen Journal*; Peter Lee Esq., Nuneaton Local History Group; Alun J. Harries Esq., Town Clerk, Eleri James, Secretary, Margaret Evans and Jenny Fox, Carmarthen Town Council; Cllr Barry Williams, T. D., mayor of Carmarthen and his consort Mrs Barbara Williams; Daniel James Esq., Ty-Gwyn Farm, Llangunnor; Revd Canon Leigh Richardson, Priest in Charge, St Peter's church; Julie Rees, secretary, The Friends of Peter's; Malcolm and Edith Lodwick, Joyce and Victor Lodwick, authors and historians, *The Story of Carmarthen*; Jewson Ltd, The Old Tinplate Works; Tony Evans, Secretary, Old Maridunians Association; Major General Talbot Rice, Regimental Lieutenant Colonel of the Welsh Guards; Colonel Tom Brown, Regimental Adjutant RHQ Welsh Guards; Lieutenant Colonel Kevin F. N. Roberts, Senior Director of Music, Welsh Guards; Carmarthen Peter's Works; CADW and last, but not least Eirlys and BBC photographer and local historian Ken 'Mayfair' Davies.

Please accept my apologies if I have inadvertently missed anyone out.